2019 Microsoft Excel®
Pivot Tables &
Introduction To Dashboards
The Step-By-Step Guide

C.J. Benton

ISBN: 9781093394832

Thank you!

Thank you for purchasing and reading this book! **Your feedback is valued and appreciated**. Please take a few minutes and leave a review.

More books by this author:

For a complete list please visit us at:
https://bentonbooks.wixsite.com/bentonbooks/buy-books

- Excel® 2019 VLOOKUP The Step-By-Step Guide
- Excel® 2016 The 30 Most Common Formulas & Features - The Step-By-Step Guide
- Excel® 2016 The VLOOKUP Formula in 30 Minutes The Step-By-Step Guide
- The Step-By-Step Guide To The VLOOKUP formula in Microsoft Excel® *(version 2013)*
- Excel® Macros & VBA For Business Users - A Beginners Guide

Questions, comments?
Please contact us at:

Email: bentontrainingbooks@gmail.com
Website: https://bentonbooks.wixsite.com/bentonbooks

TABLE OF CONTENTS

CHAPTER 1

This book can be used as a tutorial or quick reference guide. It is intended for users who are comfortable with the fundamentals of Microsoft Excel® and are now ready to build upon this skill by learning PivotTables and Dashboards.

This book assumes you already know how to create, open, save, and modify an Excel® workbook and have a general familiarity with the Excel® toolbar (Ribbon).

All of the examples in this book use **Microsoft Excel® 2019**, however most of the functionality can be applied using Microsoft Excel® version 2016. All screenshots in this book use Microsoft Excel® 2019.

While this book provides several PivotTable examples, the book does not cover ALL available Microsoft Excel® PivotTable features, formulas, and functionality.

Please always **back-up your work** and **save often**. A good best practice when attempting any new functionality is to **create a copy of the original spreadsheet** and implement your changes on the copied spreadsheet. Should anything go wrong, you then have the original spreadsheet to refer back to. Please see the diagram below.

Diagram 1:

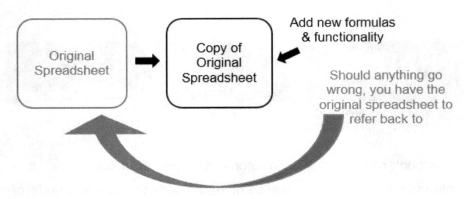

FILES FOR EXERCISES

The exercise files are available for download at the following website:
https://bentonbooks.wixsite.com/bentonbooks/excel-2019

All files are saved in **Excel® version 2019**:

- AirplaneParts.xlsx
- Autoparts_Sales_Dashbaord.xlsx
- Autoparts_Sales_Refresh_Data.xlsx
- CustomerSales.xlsx
- DashboardGraphics.xlsx
- Data_File - East_West.xlsx
- Data_File - North_South.xlsx
- EmployeeSales.csv
- FruitSales.xlsx
- MonthlySalesReport.xlsx
- Pivot_Charts.xlsx
- PoliceCrimeData.xlsx
- SocialMediaData.xlsx

CHAPTER 2

INTRODUCTION TO PIVOTTABLES

WHAT ARE PIVOTTABLES?

PivotTables are a feature within Microsoft Excel® that takes individual cells or pieces of data and lets you arrange them into numerous types of calculated views. These snapshots of summarized data, require minimal effort to create and can be changed by simply clicking or dragging fields within your report.

By using built-in functions and filters, PivotTables allow you to quickly organize and summarize large amounts of data. You can filter and drill-down for more detailed examination of your numbers and various types of analysis can be completed without the need to manually enter formulas into the spreadsheet you're analyzing.

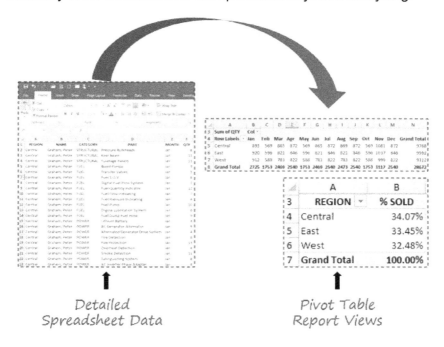

Detailed
Spreadsheet Data

Pivot Table
Report Views

For example, the below PivotTable is based on a detailed spreadsheet of 3,888 individual records containing information about airplane parts. In less than 1 minute, I was able to produce the following report for the quantity of parts sold by region:

◢	A	B	C	D	E	F	G	H	I	J	K	L	M	N
1														
2														
3	Sum of QTY_SOLD	Column Labels												
4	Row Labels	Jan	Feb	Mar	Apr	May	Jun	Jul	Aug	Sep	Oct	Nov	Dec	Grand Total
5	Central		893	569	865	872	569	865	872	869	872	569	1081	872	9768
6	East		920	596	821	846	596	821	846	821	846	596	1037	846	9592
7	West		912	588	783	822	588	783	822	783	822	588	999	822	9312
8	Grand Total		2725	1753	2469	2540	1753	2469	2540	2473	2540	1753	3117	2540	28672

These PivotTable reports can also be formatted to improve readability. However, formatting does require a little more time to complete.

Formatted example:

◢	A	B	C	D	E	F	G	H	I	J	K
1		QUARTER ▼									
2		Qtr1		Qtr2		Qtr3		Qtr4		Total Sold	Total %
3	REGION ▼	Sold	%	Sold	%	Sold	%	Sold	%		
4	Central	2,327	8.12%	2,306	8.04%	2,613	9.11%	2,522	8.80%	9,768	34.07%
5	East	2,337	8.15%	2,263	7.89%	2,513	8.76%	2,479	8.65%	9,592	33.45%
6	West	2,283	7.96%	2,193	7.65%	2,427	8.46%	2,409	8.40%	9,312	32.48%
7	TOTAL	6,947	24.23%	6,762	23.58%	7,553	26.34%	7,410	25.84%	28,672	100.00%

In today's world with the massive amounts of information available, you may be tasked with analyzing significant portions of this data. Perhaps consisting of several thousand, hundreds of thousands, or even millions of records. You may have to reconcile numbers from many different sources and formats, such as assimilating material from:

- Reports generated by another application, such as a legacy system
- Data imported into Excel® via a query from a database or other application

- Data copied or cut, and pasted into Excel® from the web or other types of screen scraping activities
- Analyzing test or research results from multiple subjects
- Integrating information due to company mergers or acquisitions

One of the easiest ways to perform various and complex types of analysis and reporting is to use PivotTables.

WHAT ARE THE MAIN PARTS OF A PIVOTTABLE?

Before we begin our first exercise, let's review the three main components of a PivotTable:

1. **Rows:** The rows section typically represents how you would like to categorize or group your data. Some examples include: employee name, region, department, part number etc.

2. **Columns:** The columns show the level or levels in which you're displaying your calculations. Often a *time period* such as a month, quarter, or year, but can also be categories, product lines, etc.

3. **Values:** Values are the calculation portion of the report, these figures can be sums, percentages, counts, averages, rankings or custom computations.

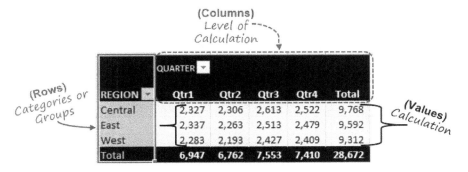

	QUARTER				
REGION	Qtr1	Qtr2	Qtr3	Qtr4	Total
Central	2,327	2,306	2,613	2,522	9,768
East	2,337	2,263	2,513	2,479	9,592
West	2,283	2,193	2,427	2,409	9,312
Total	6,947	6,762	7,553	7,410	28,672

CHAPTER 3

CREATING YOUR FIRST PIVOTTABLE

For our first exercise we'll be using a month's worth of police crime data. Below is a sample, however due to space limitations **the entire data set is not displayed**.

	A	B	C	D
1	ID	DATE	CATEGORY	AREA
2	MAR2019_01	3/1/2019	THEFT-ALL OTHER	WEST
3	MAR2019_02	3/1/2019	ROBBERY-STREET	NORTH
4	MAR2019_03	3/1/2019	NARCOTIC	WEST
5	MAR2019_04	3/1/2019	DUI	NORTH
6	MAR2019_05	3/1/2019	DUI	WEST
7	MAR2019_06	3/1/2019	AGGRAVATED ASSAULT-DV	EAST
8	MAR2019_07	3/1/2019	TRESPASS	SOUTH
9	MAR2019_08	3/1/2019	BURGLARY-RESIDENTIAL	NORTH
10	MAR2019_09	3/1/2019	BURGLARY-RESIDENTIAL	NORTH
11	MAR2019_10	3/1/2019	WEAPON	EAST
12	MAR2019_11	3/1/2019	CAR PROWL	NORTH
13	MAR2019_12	3/1/2019	THEFT-SHOPLIFT	SOUTH
14	MAR2019_13	3/1/2019	MOTOR VEHICLE THEFT	SOUTH
15	MAR2019_14	3/1/2019	ROBBERY-COMMERCIAL	NORTH
16	MAR2019_15	3/1/2019	CAR PROWL	NORTH
17	MAR2019_16	3/1/2019	TRESPASS	WEST
18	MAR2019_17	3/1/2019	BURGLARY-COMMERCIAL	EAST
19	MAR2019_18	3/1/2019	BURGLARY-COMMERCIAL-SEC	NORTH
3637	MAR2019_3636	3/31/2019	THEFT-ALL OTHER	WEST

PREPARING THE WORKSHEET

When creating PivotTables, the best practice for each worksheet to be analyzed is:

- Contain no blank rows or columns inside your dataset
- Have no merged cells
- Each column heading has a unique name

For example:

To create a basic PivotTable we'll utilize Microsoft Excel's® **'Recommended PivotTables'** feature. This tool is useful when you need to perform quick, high-level analysis, or are being asked for something ad hoc. Typically, these reports are *not* formatted or distributed to a customer.

To illustrate how this functionality works, we'll take the following spreadsheet containing police crime data and summarize:

- The total number of crimes by geographic location

For this exercise, we'll take the PoliceCrimeData.xlsx spreadsheet containing 3,636 individual crime records and counting the number of unique ID fields by Area.

The **Rows** (our grouping) will be the geographic **'AREA'** and the **Values** (our calculation) will be a **'COUNT'** of the ID records. In this demonstration we will not have a **Column** level of detail.

THE RECOMMENDED PIVOTTABLES FEATURE

Below are the steps to create a basic PivotTable using Microsoft Excel's® Recommended PivotTables Feature, to begin:

1. Open the PoliceCrimeData.xlsx spreadsheet
2. Select **columns A:D**

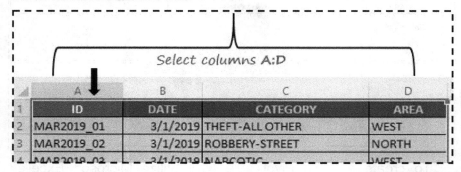

3. From the Ribbon select **Insert : Recommended PivotTables**

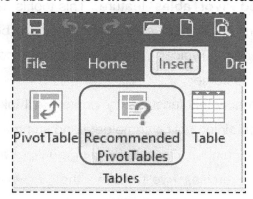

The following dialogue box will appear:

4. Select the preview for **'Count of ID by AREA'**
5. Click the '**OK**' button

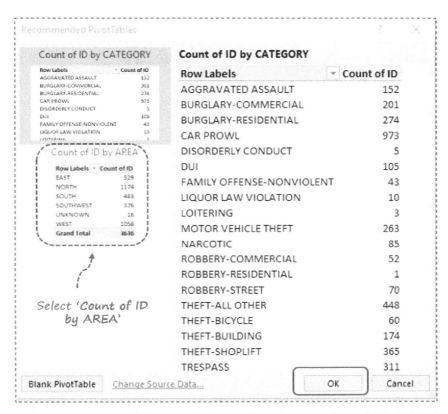

A new report will be created counting the number of ID fields by area. *Note:* this created a **new worksheet, 'Sheet1'** and the **'PivotTable Fields'** pane on the left side of the new worksheet.

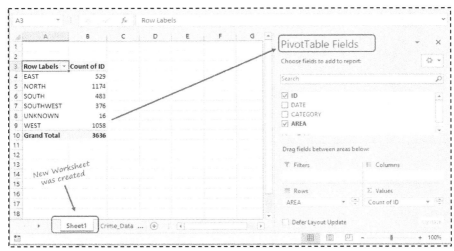

Congratulations! You created your first PivotTable! In just a few short minutes, you were able to quickly summarize the total number of crimes that occurred for a time period by geographic area.

CHAPTER 4

Let's build upon the fundamentals of creating and modifying a PivotTable, by including multiple totals, viewing the details of a specific value, and formatting our results for easier viewing.

EXAMPLE:
In this exercise we will take a spreadsheet containing fruit sale information and:

- Determine the *total* fruit sales by region and quarter
- Display the *individual* fruit sales by region and quarter

WEB ADDRESS & FILE NAME FOR EXERCISE:
https://bentonbooks.wixsite.com/bentonbooks/excel-2019
FruitSales.xlsx

SUMMARIZING DATA

Sample data for chapter 4, due to space limitations **the entire data set is not displayed**.

	A	B	C	D	E	F	G	H	I
1	REGION	SALES PERSON FIRST NAME	SALES PERSON LAST NAME	SALES PERSON ID	QUARTER	APPLES	ORANGES	MANGOS	TOTAL
2	Central	Bob	Taylor	1174	1	1,810	2,039	1,771	5,620
3	Central	Helen	Smith	833	1	102	354	59	516
4	Central	Jill	Johnson	200	1	93	322	54	469
5	Central	Sally	Morton	500	1	595	824	556	1,975
6	Central	Sam	Becker	800	1	863	1,092	824	2,779
7	East	Abbey	Williams	690	1	346	237	260	843
8	East	John	Dower	255	1	260	178	195	633
9	East	John	Wilson	300	1	286	196	215	696
10	East	Mary	Nelson	600	1	315	215	236	766
11	East	Sarah	Taylor	900	1	381	261	285	927
12	West	Alex	Steller	1000	1	163	212	127	502
13	West	Billy	Winchester	1156	1	179	234	140	552
14	West	Helen	Simpson	817	1	148	193	116	457
15	West	Jack	Smith	100	1	111	145	87	343
16	West	Joe	Tanner	400	1	122	160	96	377
17	West	Peter	Graham	700	1	134	175	105	415
18	Central	Bob	Taylor	1174	2	113	390	65	567
19	Central	Helen	Smith	833	2	1,006	1,393	940	3,338
64	West	Joe	Tanner	400	4	2,833	2,886	2,796	8,516
65	West	Peter	Graham	700	4	4,392	4,473	4,334	13,199

First, we will determine the '**total sales by region**' and then build upon this by adding the '**quarterly sales by region**':

1. Open the FruitSales.xlsx spreadsheet and select **cells 'A1:I65'**

2. From the Ribbon select **Insert : PivotTable**

The following dialogue box will appear, please note the **Data Range** and **location where the new PivotTable will be located**:

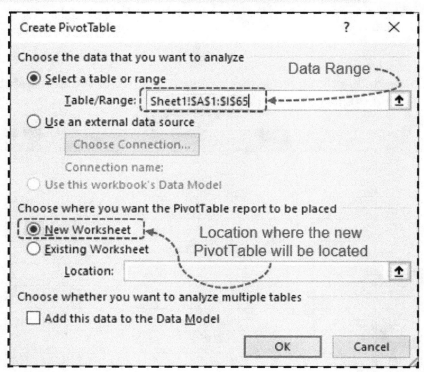

3. Click the 'OK' button

A new tab will be created and appear similar to the following. *Note: the 'PivotTable Fields' pane on the left side of the new worksheet.*

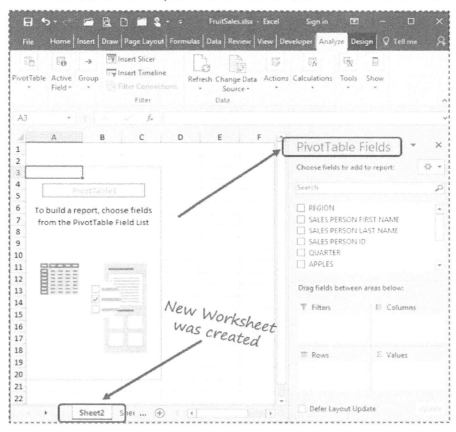

Next, we'll **categorize** our report and select a **calculation** value.

4. In the ***'PivotTable Fields' pane*** select the following fields:
   - **REGION** *(Rows section)*
   - **TOTAL** *(∑ Values section)*

Please see image on next page, for a screenshot of step #4

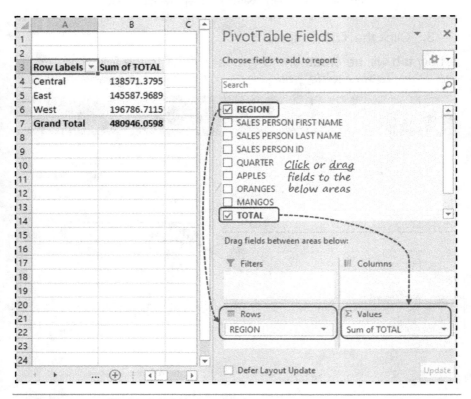

WHY DO THE 'Σ VALUES' FIELDS SOMETIMES DEFAULT TO *COUNT* INSTEAD OF *SUM*?

When PivotTable source data contains blank rows, for example when selecting the entire column such as (Sheet1!$A:$I) instead of a specific cell rage (Sheet1!$A$1:$I$65), Excel® will default the calculation of a field added to the 'Σ **Values**' section to **count** instead of **sum**.

If this happens, to change the 'Σ **Values**' section from **count** to **sum**:

1. Click the '**Count of TOTAL**' drop-down arrow, then from the sub-menu select '**Value Field Settings…**'

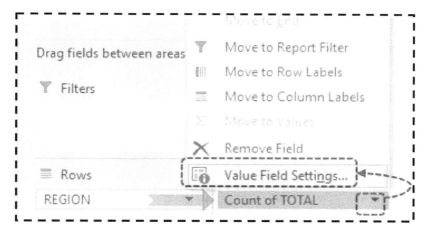

The following **'Value Field Settings…'** dialogue box will appear:

2. From the **'Summarize value field by'** list, select the **'Sum'** option

3. Click the **'OK'** button

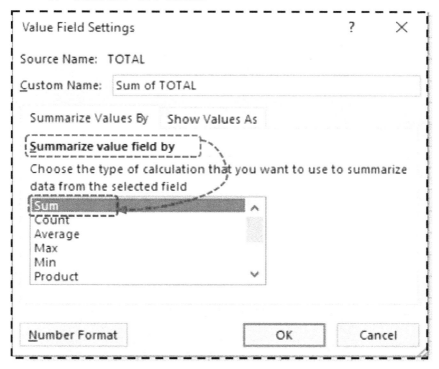

Continuing with our example:

The following should be displayed on the right side of your screen
Note: the format is not very easy to read.

	A	B
1		
2		
3	Row Labels ▾	Sum of TOTAL
4	Central	138571.3795
5	East	145587.9689
6	West	196786.7115
7	**Grand Total**	**480946.0598**

5. We can change the column labels and format of the numbers. In the below example:

   ▪ Select cell **'A3'** and change the text from **'Row Labels'** to **'REGION'**

   ▪ Select cell **'B3'** and change the text from **'Sum of TOTAL'** to **'TOTAL SALES'**

   ▪ You may also change the currency format in cells **'B4:B7'**. In the below example, the format was changed to U.S. dollars with *zero* decimal places

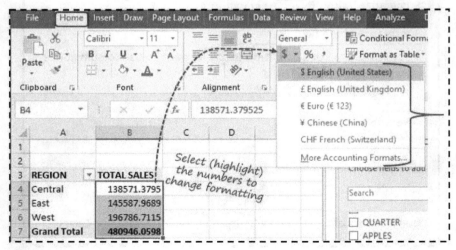

Below is the formatted example:

	A	B
1		
2		
3	REGION ▼	TOTAL SALES
4	Central	$ 138,571
5	East	$ 145,588
6	West	$ 196,787
7	Grand Total	$ 480,946

To enhance the report further we're going to going add *Quarter columns*. This "level" dimension will provide greater detail of the total fruit sales.

6. Inside the *'PivotTable Fields' pane* **drag** the **'QUARTER'** field to the **'Columns'** section.

IMPORTANT!
Excel® is reading the **'Quarter'** as a numeric value, therefore if you click, **instead of drag** the field to the 'Columns' section, Excel® will apply a calculation.   If this happens, click the drop-down arrow for **'Sum of QUARTER'** in the **'Σ Values'** section and select the option **'Move to Column Labels'**

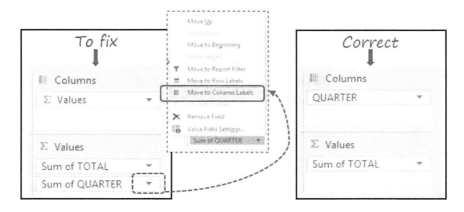

17

We now have **'QUARTER'** added to the summary

    7.   Select cell **'B3'** and change the text from **'Column Labels'** to **'BY QUARTER'**

    8.   The labels for cells **'B4'**, **'C4'**, **'D4'**, & **'E4'** were changed by adding the abbreviation text **'QTR'** in front of each quarter number

Before *formatting:*

◢	A	B	C	D	E	F
1						
2						
3	TOTAL SALES	Column Labels ▾				
4	REGION ▾	1	2	3	4	Grand Total
5	Central	$ 11,359	$ 19,352	$ 34,097	$ 73,763	$ 138,571
6	East	$ 3,865	$ 19,343	$ 38,811	$ 83,569	$ 145,588
7	West	$ 2,646	$ 23,586	$ 42,590	$ 127,964	$ 196,787
8	Grand Total	$ 17,870	$ 62,281	$ 115,499	$ 285,296	$ 480,946

After *formatting:*

TOTAL SALES	BY QUARTER ▾				
REGION ▾	QTR 1	QTR 2	QTR 3	QTR 4	Grand Total
Central	$ 11,359	$ 19,352	$ 34,097	$ 73,763	$ 138,571
East	$ 3,865	$ 19,343	$ 38,811	$ 83,569	$ 145,588
West	$ 2,646	$ 23,586	$ 42,590	$ 127,964	$ 196,787
Grand Total	$ 17,870	$ 62,281	$ 115,499	$ 285,296	$ 480,946

HOW TO DRILL-DOWN PIVOTTABLE DATA

Before continuing with our example, let's say you wanted to investigate further why the *Central Region's Q1 results* are so much higher than the East & West regions.

TOTAL SALES	BY QUARTER ▾
REGION ▾	QTR 1
Central	$ 11,359
East	$ 3,865
West	$ 2,646
Grand Total	$ 17,870

PivotTables allow you to **double-click** **on any calculated value to see the detail of that cell**. By double clicking the value, this will create a *new worksheet* containing an Excel® *table* with the details of that cell.

- For example, double-click on the calculated value in cell **'B5'**

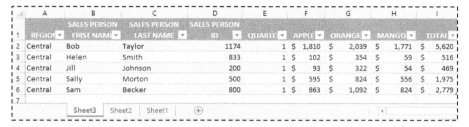

- To delete the table, **right-click** on **'Sheet3'** and select **'Delete'**

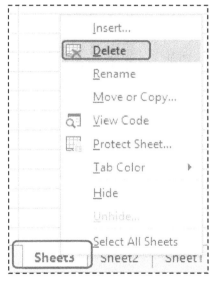

- You'll receive the following message, click the **'Delete'** button

ADDING ADDITIONAL ROWS (CATEGORIES) TO YOUR PIVOTTABLE

Lastly, we'll review how to display the individual fruit sales by region and quarter.

9. Drag the **'QUARTER'** field from the **'COLUMNS'** section to the **'ROWS'** section.

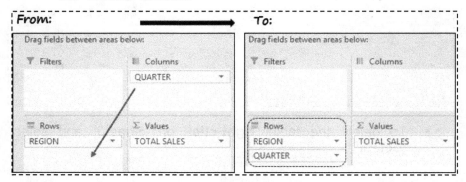

10. Drag the fields **'APPLES'**, **'ORANGES'**, & **'MANGOS'** to the **'∑ *Values*'** section of the **'PivotTable Fields'** pane, place the fruit fields *before* the **'TOTAL SALES'** value

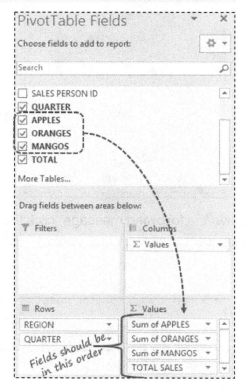

The results should look similar to the following:

REGION ▼	Sum of APPLES	Sum of ORANGES	Sum of MANGOS	TOTAL SALES
⊟ Central	$ 43,481	$ 53,278	$ 41,812	$ 138,571
QTR 1	$ 3,463	$ 4,631	$ 3,264	$ 11,359
QTR 2	$ 5,992	$ 7,652	$ 5,709	$ 19,352
QTR 3	$ 10,634	$ 13,280	$ 10,183	$ 34,097
QTR 4	$ 23,392	$ 27,715	$ 22,656	$ 73,763
⊟ East	$ 50,626	$ 47,117	$ 47,845	$ 145,588
QTR 1	$ 1,587	$ 1,087	$ 1,190	$ 3,865
QTR 2	$ 6,891	$ 6,149	$ 6,303	$ 19,343
QTR 3	$ 13,583	$ 12,502	$ 12,726	$ 38,811
QTR 4	$ 28,564	$ 27,380	$ 27,625	$ 83,569
⊟ West	$ 69,750	$ 65,259	$ 61,778	$ 196,787
QTR 1	$ 856	$ 1,119	$ 671	$ 2,646
QTR 2	$ 7,819	$ 8,253	$ 7,513	$ 23,586
QTR 3	$ 15,335	$ 14,074	$ 13,182	$ 42,590
QTR 4	$ 45,739	$ 41,813	$ 40,411	$ 127,964
Grand Total	$ 163,857	$ 165,655	$ 151,435	$ 480,946

CHAPTER 5

DISPLAYING PERCENTAGES IN PIVOTTABLES

Another great benefit of using PivotTables is the ability to display numbers in various descriptive formats. In this chapter we'll explore how to use *percentages*.

EXAMPLE:
You're an analyst and need to determine:

- The percentage of Airplane Parts sold by Region

- The percentage of Airplane Parts sold by Category and Region

WEB ADDRESS & FILE NAME FOR EXERCISE:
https://bentonbooks.wixsite.com/bentonbooks/excel-2019
AirplaneParts.xlsx

Sample data for this chapter, due to space limitations **the entire data set is not displayed**.

	A	B	C	D	E	F
1	REGION	NAME	CATEGORY	PART	EOM_DATE	QTY
2	Central	Graham, Peter	STRUCTURAL	Pressure Bulkheads	31 January 2020	8
3	Central	Graham, Peter	STRUCTURAL	Keel Beam	31 January 2020	11
4	Central	Graham, Peter	STRUCTURAL	Fuselage Panels	31 January 2020	13
5	Central	Graham, Peter	FUEL	Boost Pumps	31 January 2020	9
6	Central	Graham, Peter	FUEL	Transfer Valves	31 January 2020	5
7	Central	Graham, Peter	FUEL	Fuel S.O.V.	31 January 2020	6
8	Central	Graham, Peter	FUEL	Digital Fuel Flow System	31 January 2020	7
9	Central	Graham, Peter	FUEL	Fuel Quantity Indicator	31 January 2020	12
10	Central	Graham, Peter	FUEL	Fuel Flow Indicating	31 January 2020	7
11	Central	Graham, Peter	FUEL	Fuel Pressure Indicating	31 January 2020	4
12	Central	Graham, Peter	FUEL	Fuel Pump	31 January 2020	10
13	Central	Graham, Peter	FUEL	Engine Lubrication System	31 January 2020	6
14	Central	Graham, Peter	FUEL	Fuel Dump Fuel Hose	31 January 2020	9
15	Central	Graham, Peter	POWER	Lithium Battery	31 January 2020	4
16	Central	Graham, Peter	POWER	AC Generator-Alternator	31 January 2020	9
17	Central	Graham, Peter	POWER	Alternator/Generator Drive System	31 January 2020	4
18	Central	Graham, Peter	POWER	Fire Detection	31 January 2020	8
19	Central	Graham, Peter	POWER	Fire Protection	31 January 2020	13
20	Central	Graham, Peter	POWER	Overheat Detection	31 January 2020	4
3889	West	Winchester, Charles	WING	Engine Mounts	31 December 2019	11

Create a new PivotTable report, to see screenshot illustrations of steps #1 - #3, please see chapter 4 Basic PivotTable Functionality, page 12:

1. Open the AirplaneParts.xlsx spreadsheet and select **cells A1:F3889**

2. From the Ribbon select **Insert : PivotTable**

3. Click the '**OK**' button

A new tab will be created and the *'PivotTable Fields' pane* should appear on the left side of your screen.

4. In the *'PivotTable Fields' pane* select the following fields:
   - **REGION** *(Rows section)*
   - **QTY** *(∑ Values section)*

A report similar to the following should be displayed:

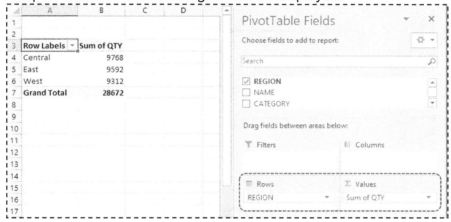

5. Click the '**Sum of QTY**' drop-down arrow, then from the sub-menu select '**Value Field Settings…**'

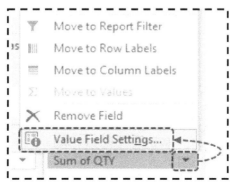

From the following dialogue box:

6. Select the *tab* **'Show Values As'**

7. From the '**Show values as**' drop-down list select **'% of Grand Total'**

8. In the field '**Custom Name:**' change to **% of QTY**

9. Click the **'OK'** button

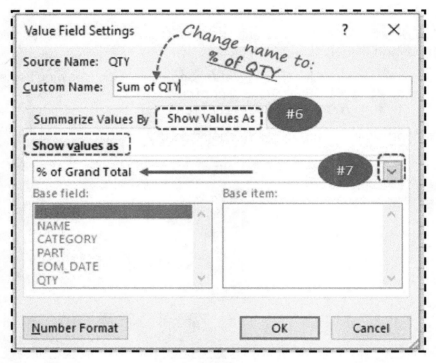

The quantities by Region have been changed to a percentage.

Row Labels	% of QTY
Central	34.07%
East	33.45%
West	32.48%
Grand Total	100.00%

IMPORTANT!

In Excel®, often percentages when summed together *may exceed or not equal 100%*, this is due to Excel® rounding the percentages either up or down.

We've now answered the question, what is the percentage of Airplane Parts sold by Region.

To determine the percentage of Airplane Parts sold by Region _and_ Category:

> 10. In the *'PivotTable Fields' pane* click the following field:
>   - CATEGORY *(Rows section)*

Let's improve the readability of the report

> 11. Select cells **'B4:B19',** from the Ribbon, select **Home** and in the **'Number'** section reduce the decimal place by two points

> 12. Select cell **'A3'** and change the text from '**Row Labels**' to **'Sales By Region'**

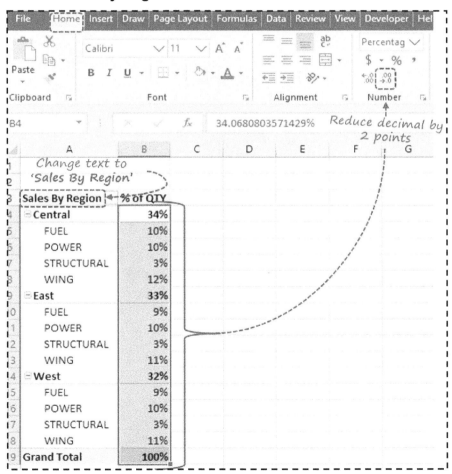

The report is displaying the total by Region with the Region name located at the top for each grouping, this is difficult to read as our eye naturally looks to the bottom when summing totals. To address this:

13. Select cell **'A3'** and from the **PivotTable Tools** Ribbon select the **'Design'** tab

14. Select the **'Subtotals'** drop-down arrow and then the option **'Show all Subtotals at <u>B</u>ottom of Group'**

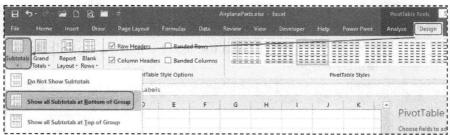

From:

	A	B
3	Sales By Region ▾	% of QTY
4	⊟Central	34%
5	FUEL	10%
6	POWER	10%
7	STRUCTURAL	3%
8	WING	12%
9	⊟East	33%
10	FUEL	9%
11	POWER	10%
12	STRUCTURAL	3%
13	WING	11%
14	⊟West	32%
15	FUEL	9%
16	POWER	10%
17	STRUCTURAL	3%
18	WING	11%
19	Grand Total	100%

To:

	A	B
3	Sales By Region ▾	% of QTY
4	⊟Central	
5	FUEL	10%
6	POWER	10%
7	STRUCTURAL	3%
8	WING	12%
9	Central Total	34%
10	⊟East	
11	FUEL	9%
12	POWER	10%
13	STRUCTURAL	3%
14	WING	11%
15	East Total	33%
16	⊟West	
17	FUEL	9%
18	POWER	10%
19	STRUCTURAL	3%
20	WING	11%
21	West Total	32%
22	Grand Total	100%

CHAPTER 6

GROUPING PIVOTTABLE DATA

While PivotTables are excellent at summarizing information, there may be times when you have a lot of detailed individual records such as customer demographics, sales, locations, etc. With this type of data granularity, often more insight can be gained when you can cluster these records into categories or ranges. To complete this type of of segmented analysis we can utilize the **'Grouping'** feature.

EXAMPLE:
You received a large amount of *detailed* customer records and need to:
- Group the number of customers by how much they spent
- The percentage each segment to the overall sales total

WEB ADDRESS & FILE NAME FOR EXERCISE:
https://bentonbooks.wixsite.com/bentonbooks/excel-2019
CustomerSales.xlsx

Sample data for this chapter, due to space limitations **the entire data set is not displayed**.

	A	B
1	CUSTOMER ID	AMOUNT PURCHASED
2	111	$142
3	222	$153
4	333	$442
5	444	$409
6	555	$136
7	666	$147
8	777	$436
9	888	$403
10	999	$1,500
31	3330	$752

GROUPING RECORDS

Create a new PivotTable report, to see screenshot illustrations of steps #1 - #3, please see chapter 4 Basic PivotTable Functionality, page 12:

1. Open the CustomerSales.xlsx spreadsheet and select **cells 'A1:B31'**
2. From the Ribbon select **Insert : PivotTable**
3. Click the '**OK**' button

A new tab will be created and the *'PivotTable Fields' pane* should appear on the left side of your screen.

4. In the *'PivotTable Fields' pane* **drag** the following fields:
   - **AMOUNT PURCHASED** *(Rows section)*
   - **CUSTOMER ID** *twice* *(∑ Values section)*

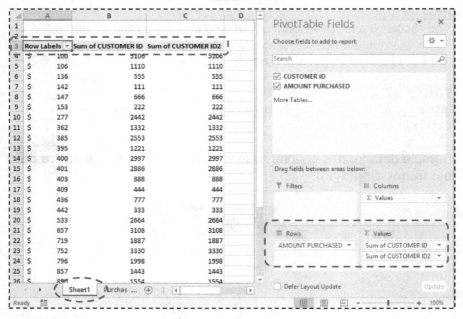

5. Click cell '**A4**'

28

6. From the **PivotTable Tools** Ribbon select the tab **Analyze :
Group Field**

The following dialogue box will appear:

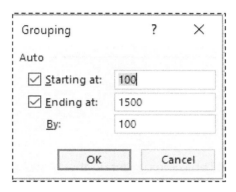

7. Verify both the **'Starting at:'** and **'Ending at:'** check boxes
   are checked:
   ▪ **'Starting at:'** will default to 100 (this is the *lowest value*
     in the dataset)

   ▪ **'Ending at:'** will default to 1500 (this is the *highest value*
     in the dataset)

   ▪ Enter **100** in the '**By:**' field *(this is the amount between
     group segments)*

8. Click the **'OK'** button

We've now grouped customer purchase amounts into segments, with
each bracket differential representing approximately 100.

However, this table is not providing meaningful information, because
it is incorrectly summing **'CUSTOMER ID'**, to fix this:

Row Labels ▼	Sum of CUSTOMER ID	Sum of CUSTOMER ID2
100-199	7770	7770
200-299	2442	2442
300-399	5106	5106
400-499	8325	8325
500-599	2664	2664
600-699	3108	3108
700-799	7215	7215
800-899	2997	2997
900-999	3219	3219
1000-1099	4329	4329
1100-1199	3441	3441
1400-1500	999	999
Grand Total	**51615**	**51615**

Purchase Segments

Incorrectly Summing Customer ID

9. In the 'PivotTable Fields' list, in the '∑ *Values section'*, click the drop-down arrow for the *first* 'Sum of CUSTOMER ID'

10. Select the 'Value Field Settings...'option

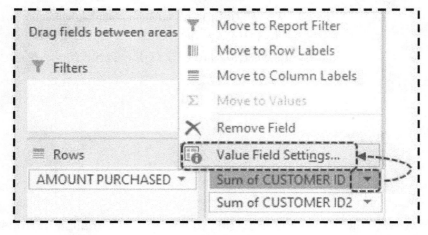

COUNT FUNCTION

The count function returns the number of times a specific value has been found in a particular range.

In our example, we're counting the number of customers who made purchases within a certain price point.

11. In the '**Summarize value field by**' list box select '**Count**'

12. In the '**Custom Name:**' field change to '**NUMBER OF CUSTOMERS**'

13. Click the '**OK**' button

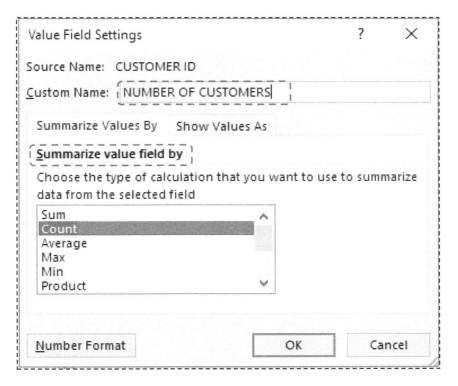

14. In the '**PivotTable Fields**' list, in the '∑ *Values section*', click the drop-down arrow for the _second_ '**Sum of CUSTOMER ID**'

15. Select the '**Value Field Settings...**'option

16. In the '**Summarize value field by**' list select '**Count**'

17. In the '**Custom Name:**' field change to '**% OF CUSTOMERS**'

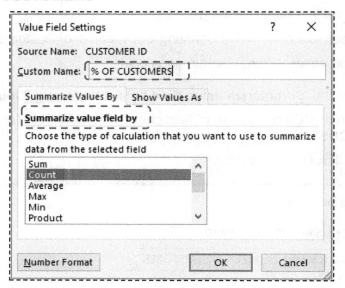

18. Click the '**Show Values As**' tab

19. Click the '**Show values as**' drop-down arrow and select '**% of Grand Total**'

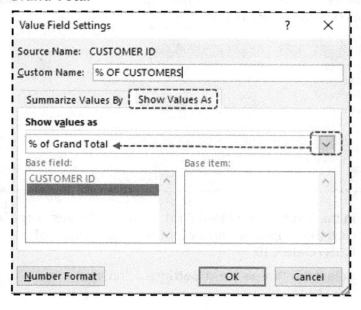

20. Click the **'OK'** button

21. Change the text in cell '**A3**' from 'Row Labels' to '**AMOUNT PURCHASED**'

We now have a report that groups the number of customers by how much they spent and each purchase group's percentage of the overall sales total.

	AMOUNT PURCHASED ▾	NUMBER OF CUSTOMERS	% OF CUSTOMERS
3			
4	100-199	7	23.33%
5	200-299	1	3.33%
6	300-399	3	10.00%
7	400-499	6	20.00%
8	500-599	1	3.33%
9	600-699	1	3.33%
10	700-799	3	10.00%
11	800-899	2	6.67%
12	900-999	1	3.33%
13	1000-1099	2	6.67%
14	1100-1199	2	6.67%
15	1400-1500	1	3.33%
16	**Grand Total**	30	100.00%

CHAPTER 7

SLICERS, TIMELINES, & FILTERING

Excel® offers a number of filtering options, in this chapter we'll examine some of the most commonly used.

The first two are graphical and provide an easy and intuitive way for your reporting to be interactive, these are:

- **Timeline:** is a *slider or button filter* allowing users to quickly categorize *individual date values* into months, quarters, or years.

- **Slicers** are *button filters* and allow the user to filter by selecting one or more text values.

These Timelines and Slicers may be used in combination with one another and are ideal for analysts or customers who like to examine data from many different perspectives.

This chapter concludes by reviewing a few of the built-in conditional filters, these include how to quickly identify top & bottom performers, and return only records that meet a specific numeric threshold, or text.

EXAMPLE:

You're a Financial Analyst that supports a manufacturing company of aerospace parts. You've been asked to attend an impromptu sales meeting for Regional Managers. The agenda <u>has not</u> been determined, instead you've been asked to prepare the sales data for the last 12 months and answer questions as they arise. Since you're unsure of what the managers will ask, you decide to create a PivotTable report with a Timeline and a category Slicer.

WEB ADDRESS & FILE NAME FOR EXERCISE:
https://bentonbooks.wixsite.com/bentonbooks/excel-2019
AirplaneParts.xlsx

Sample data for this chapter, due to space limitations **the entire data set is not displayed**. *Note: Column 'E' is a date value.*

	A	B	C	D	E	F
1	REGION	NAME	CATEGORY	PART	EOM_DATE	QTY
2	Central	Graham, Peter	STRUCTURAL	Pressure Bulkheads	31 January 2020	8
3	Central	Graham, Peter	STRUCTURAL	Keel Beam	31 January 2020	11
4	Central	Graham, Peter	STRUCTURAL	Fuselage Panels	31 January 2020	13
5	Central	Graham, Peter	FUEL	Boost Pumps	31 January 2020	9
6	Central	Graham, Peter	FUEL	Transfer Valves	31 January 2020	5
7	Central	Graham, Peter	FUEL	Fuel S.O.V.	31 January 2020	6
8	Central	Graham, Peter	FUEL	Digital Fuel Flow System	31 January 2020	7
9	Central	Graham, Peter	FUEL	Fuel Quantity Indicator	31 January 2020	12
10	Central	Graham, Peter	FUEL	Fuel Flow Indicating	31 January 2020	7
11	Central	Graham, Peter	FUEL	Fuel Pressure Indicating	31 January 2020	4
12	Central	Graham, Peter	FUEL	Fuel Pump	31 January 2020	10
13	Central	Graham, Peter	FUEL	Engine Lubrication System	31 January 2020	6
14	Central	Graham, Peter	FUEL	Fuel Dump Fuel Hose	31 January 2020	9
15	Central	Graham, Peter	POWER	Lithium Battery	31 January 2020	4
16	Central	Graham, Peter	POWER	AC Generator-Alternator	31 January 2020	9
17	Central	Graham, Peter	POWER	Alternator/Generator Drive System	31 January 2020	4
18	Central	Graham, Peter	POWER	Fire Detection	31 January 2020	8
19	Central	Graham, Peter	POWER	Fire Protection	31 January 2020	13
20	Central	Graham, Peter	POWER	Overheat Detection	31 January 2020	4
3889	West	Winchester, Charles	WING	Engine Mounts	31 December 2019	11

TIMELINE

Create a new PivotTable report, to see screenshot illustrations of steps #1 - #3, please see chapter 4 Basic PivotTable Functionality, page 12:

1. Open the AirplaneParts.xlsx spreadsheet and select **cells 'A1:F3889'**

2. From the Ribbon select **Insert : PivotTable**

3. Click the '**OK**' button

A new tab will be created and the *'PivotTable Fields' pane* should appear on the left side of your screen.

4. In the *'PivotTable Fields' pane* select the following fields:
    - REGION *(Rows section)*
    - CATEGORY *(Rows section)*
    - QTY *(∑ Values section)*

IMPORTANT!
In order for a Timeline to be used all the data in the date column must **be formatted as a date.**

In this example, once we click the field **'EOM_DATE'** Excel® will create the additional calendar options **Quarters** & **Years**.

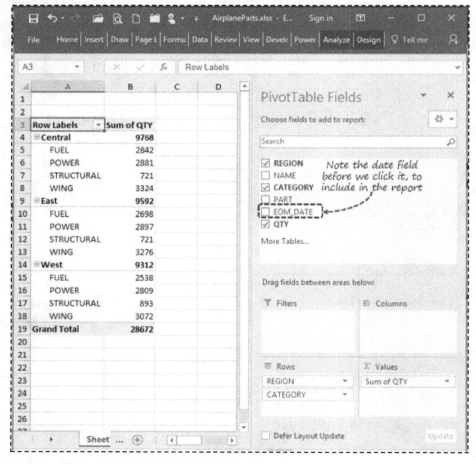

5. Click the field **'EOM_DATE'**

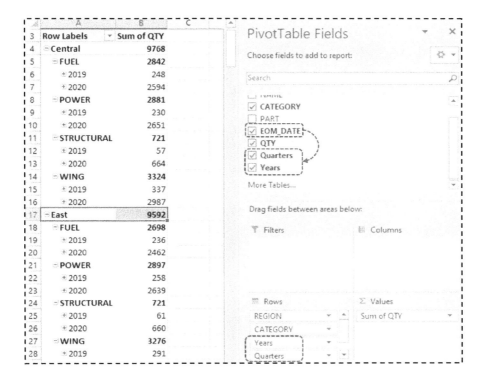

As you can see, Excel® has now created fields for **Quarters** & **Years**, however this type of display isn't very helpful. The Financial Analyst won't be able to quickly answer very many questions. Before adding the Timeline, let's re-arrange the PivotTable report to be more user friendly.

6. In the *'PivotTable Fields'* pane **uncheck** the following fields:
   ▪ Quarters *(Rows section)*
   ▪ Years *(Rows section)*

7. Drag the field **'EOM_DATE'** to the **'Columns'** section

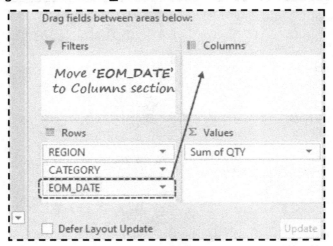

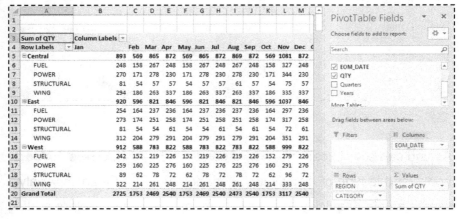

8. Insert 8 blank rows above row 3

9. Select cell **'A14'**, then from the **PivotTable Tools** Ribbon select the tab **Analyze : Insert Timeline**

You'll receive the following prompt:

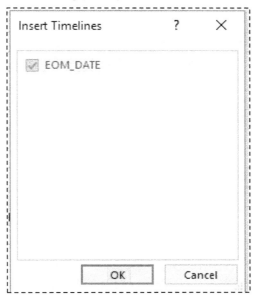

10. Click the **'EOM_DATE'** checkbox and then the **'OK'** button

11. The following **Timeline** should now appear, *drag to the area near cell* **'A1'**

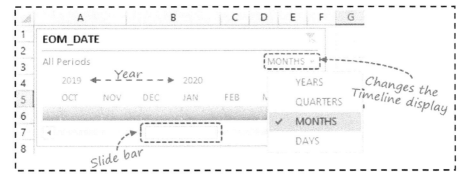

Tryout how the calculated views change by selecting individual months. For example, select Jan 2020 and Feb 2020.

	A	B	C	D
1	EOM_DATE			
2				
3	Jan - Feb 2020			MONTHS ▾
4	2020			
5	)EC JAN FEB MAR	APR	MAY	JUN
6				
7	◄			►
8				
9	Sum of QTY	Column Labels ▾		
10	Row Labels ▾	Jan	Feb	Grand Total
11	⊟ Central	893	569	1462
12	FUEL	248	158	406
13	POWER	270	171	441
14	STRUCTURAL	81	54	135
15	WING	294	186	480
16	⊟ East	920	596	1516
17	FUEL	254	164	418

Example of changing the Timeline Display from **Months** to **Quarters**

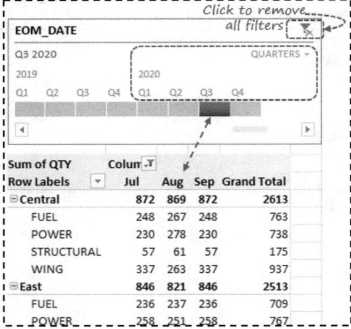

Click to remove all filters

EOM_DATE				
Q3 2020			QUARTERS ▾	
2019		2020		
Q1 Q2 Q3 Q4	Q1 Q2 Q3 Q4			
◄			►	

Sum of QTY	Colun ▾			
Row Labels ▾	Jul	Aug	Sep	Grand Total
⊟ Central	872	869	872	2613
FUEL	248	267	248	763
POWER	230	278	230	738
STRUCTURAL	57	61	57	175
WING	337	263	337	937
⊟ East	846	821	846	2513
FUEL	236	237	236	709
POWER	258	251	258	767

SLICER

1. Select cell **'A14'**, then from the **PivotTable Tools** Ribbon select the tab **Analyze : Insert Slicer**

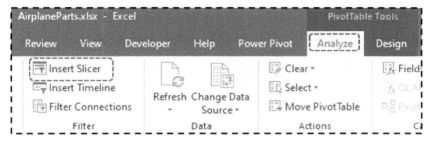

You'll receive the following prompt:

2. Click the **'CATEGORY'** checkbox and then the **'OK'** button

3. The following slicer should now appear, *drag to the area near cell* **'G1'**

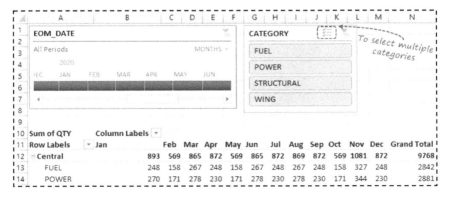

The Financial Analyst may now answer all types of questions, with just a few clicks and without having to manually re-sort or add/remove formulas. Here are some examples:

- What are the total *Fuel* sales for **Feb 2020**?
- In the last 12 months, what are the **combined** sales for only the *Structural & Wing* categories?
- Provide the **2020 Q3** sales for *Power*

REPORT CONNECTIONS

Report connections allow you to connect Timelines and/or Slicers to multiple PivotTables. To see a detailed example of how this functionality works, please see 'Chapter 14 Auto Parts Dashboard, pages 154 - 156'.

FORMATTING TIMELINES & SLICERS

To change the ***display name*** of either a Timeline or Slicer:

1. Select either the Timeline or Slicer

2. From the **Timeline** or **Slicer Tools** Ribbon, select **'Options'**

3. Select either the **'Timeline Caption' or 'Slicer Caption'** box and enter a new name

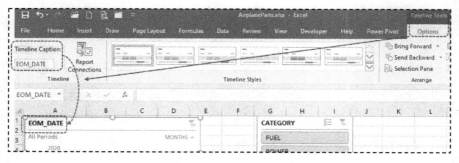

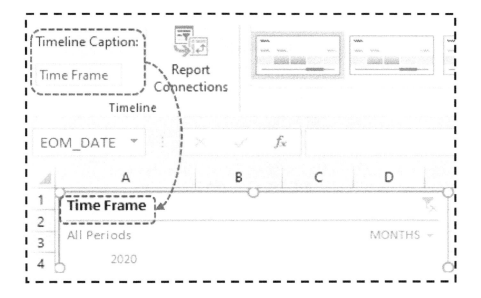

To change the **Style format** of a Timeline or Slicer:

1. Select either the Timeline or Slicer

2. From the **Timeline** or **Slicer Tools** Ribbon, select **'Options'**

3. Select either the **'Timeline Styles' or 'Slicer Styles'** drop-down menu and select a new style

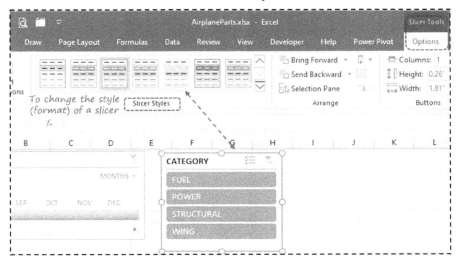

UNGROUPING DATE DATA

While having the date fields *Month, Quarter, & Year* automatically be added to our 'PivotTable Fields' list is helpful, there still may be times when you want to have the **individual dates** included in your report. Using our current example:

1. Remove all Timeline and Slicer filters, so all months and categories are being displayed

2. Select cell **'A14'** and from the *'PivotTable Fields' pane* **uncheck** fields **'REGION'** & **'CATEGORY'**

3. Drag the **'EOM_DATE'** field from the **'Columns'** section to the **'Rows'** section

4. Select any month, then from the **PivotTable Tools** Ribbon select the tab **Analyze : Ungroup**

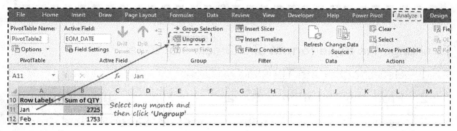

The individual dates should now be displayed:

	A	B
10	Row Labels	Sum of QTY
11	31 December 2019	2540
12	31 January 2020	2725
13	28 February 2020	1753
14	31 March 2020	2469
15	30 April 2020	2540
16	31 May 2020	1753
17	30 June 2020	2469
18	31 July 2020	2540
19	31 August 2020	2473
20	30 September 2020	2540
21	31 October 2020	1753
22	30 November 2020	3117
23	**Grand Total**	**28672**

CONDITIONAL FILTERS

In the first part of this chapter we reviewed how Timelines and Slicers may be used for interactive filtering. In this section, we'll demonstrate how to use built-in PivotTable filtering for **specific conditions**. If you're familiar with Excel's conditional formatting capabilities, this is very similar.

EXAMPLE:

In the airplane parts spreadsheet, if we wanted to know:
- The *top 10* airplane parts sold by category?
- The *bottom 10* airplane parts sold by category?
- The *top 10* airplane parts sold by Quarter?
- How many parts sold more than 800 in quantity?

VALUE FILTERS (TOP & BOTTOM PERFORMERS)

1. Open the AirplaneParts.xlsx spreadsheet and select **cells 'A1:F3889'**

2. From the Ribbon select **Insert : PivotTable**

3. Click the '**OK**' button

A new tab will be created and the *'PivotTable Fields' pane* should appear on the left side of your screen.

4. In the *'PivotTable Fields' pane* select the following fields:
   - **CATEGORY** *(Columns section)*
   - **PART** *(Rows section)*
   - **QTY** *(Σ Values section)*

5. Select cell '**A4**' and click the drop-down arrow of '**Row Labels**'

6. From the menu select '**Value Filters**' then '**Top 10…**'

7. The following prompt will appear, click the **'OK'** button

The following will be the result, you may *change the quantity from 10 to any number you would like to see.*

Sum of QTY	Colum ▼				
Row Labels	⊤ FUEL	POWER	STRUCTURAL	WING	Grand Total
Auxilliary Structure				949	949
Boost Pumps	841				841
Digital Fuel Flow System	841				841
Engine Lubrication System	849				849
Engine Struts				901	901
Fire Detection		837			837
Fire Protection		1065			1065
Fuel Dump Fuel Hose	881				881
Keel Beam			857		857
Wing Webs				849	849
Grand Total	3412	1902	857	2699	8870

Similarly, we may change to show the *bottom 10*.

8. Select cell **'A4'** and click the drop-down arrow of **'Row Labels'**

9. From the menu select '**V**alue Filters' then '**T**op 10…'

10. The following prompt will appear, click the drop-down arrow that says '**Top**' and change to '**Bottom**'

11. Click the '**OK**' button

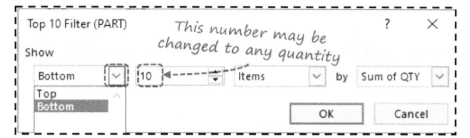

The following will be the result, you may *change the quantity from 10 to any number you would like to see.*

Sum of QTY	Colur ▾				
Row Labels	⊤ FUEL	POWER	STRUCTURAL	WING	Grand Total
AC Generator-Alternator		653			653
AC Inverter Phase Adapter		741			741
Engine Mounts				705	705
Extinguishing System		709			709
Fuel Flow Indicating	741				741
Fuselage Panels			701		701
NAC/Pylon Wing Fitting				729	729
Overheat Detection		721			721
Smoke Detection		701			701
Transfer Valves	709				709
Grand Total	1450	3525	701	1434	7110

You may a add a Timeline *(see page 35 for instructions)* to quickly see the *top or bottom 10 by* time frames.

Let's review another example, this time we'll specify the quantity.

1. Select cell '**A4**' and click the drop-down arrow of '**Row Labels**'

2. From the menu select **'Value Filters'** then **'Greater Than Or Equal To…'**

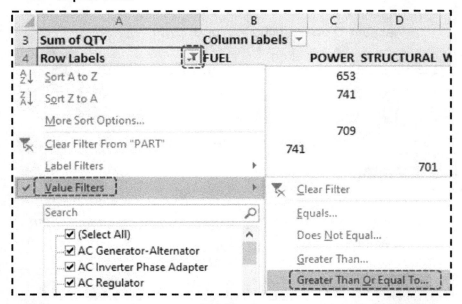

3. The following prompt will appear, enter the number **800** in the field after the drop-down box *'is greater than or equal to'*

4. Click the **'OK'** button

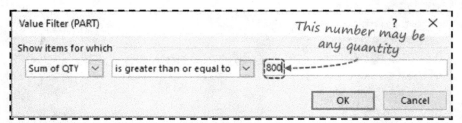

The following will be the result:

Sum of QTY	Colur ˅				
Row Labels	⊤ FUEL	POWER	STRUCTURAL	WING	Grand Total
Alternator/Generator Drive System		805			805
Auxilliary Structure				949	949
Boost Pumps	841				841
Bulkheads				801	801
Digital Fuel Flow System	841				841
Engine Lubrication System	849				849
Engine Struts				901	901
Fire Detection		837			837
Fire Protection		1065			1065
Fuel Dump Fuel Hose	881				881
Fuel Pressure Indicating	817				817
Fuel S.O.V.	821				821
Keel Beam			857		857
Lithium Battery		801			801
Longeron/Stringers				809	809
Panels				805	805
Spars				817	817
Wing Webs				849	849
Grand Total	5050	3508	857	5931	15346

REMOVING FILTERS

To **remove a filter**:

1. Select cell **'A4'** and click the drop-down arrow of **'Row Labels'**

2. From the menu select **Clear Filter From** "`<filter value will be listed here>`"

49

CHAPTER 8

PivotTables provide an excellent way to summarize large amounts of data in a numeric table-layout. Pivot *Charts* make your analysis even more effective by presenting the information in graphical form.

In this chapter, we'll explore four of the most common PivotChart types; *Bar, Column, Pie* and *Line*. These charts fall into two main categories; 1) comparison and 2) trend.

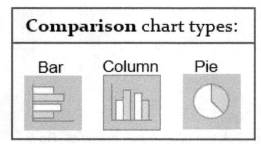
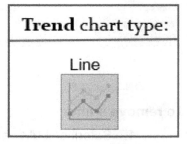

Bar and *Column* charts are best for comparing numbers, such as currency or quantity. *Column* charts display data vertically, and are a better choice if your data includes <u>negative values</u>.

Pie charts also compare data and are ideal for illustrating percentages as part of the whole, for example sales or product <u>allocation</u>.

Line charts are used to demonstrate <u>changes over a period of time</u> and are helpful in understanding trends. Often used when studying financial or frequency figures.

Irrespective of the chart type used, it's important to be mindful of *the number of elements you're displaying* and *the use of colors*. If there are too many, your charts will be become ambiguous and difficult to read, especially if your customer is viewing a black and white print out of your chart.

Similarly, if your chart is part of a presentation being projected, audience members sitting farther back from the screen will have a hard time seeing more than 4 – 5 chart values or distinguishing between subtle color differences.

EXAMPLES:

IMPORTANT!
The following four examples focus on how to use Pivot Charts. To aid in the learning process, **the PivotTables have already been created**.

WEB ADDRESS & FILE NAME FOR EXERCISE:
https://bentonbooks.wixsite.com/bentonbooks/excel-2019
Pivot_Charts.xlsx

PIE CHART EXAMPLE

For our first example, you're an analyst and want to understand if crimes are occurring more often in a particular area of the county.

1. Open the Pivot_Charts.xlsx spreadsheet and select the worksheet **'Pie Chart'**

2. From the Ribbon select **PivotTable Tools : Analyze** and then the **PivotChart** icon

IMPORTANT!
If you do not see the *PivotTable Tools : Analyze* option on your Ribbon, click any PivotTable cell. This option only appears when a PivotTable field is active.

3. Select **'Pie'** from the dialogue box
4. Click the **'OK'** button

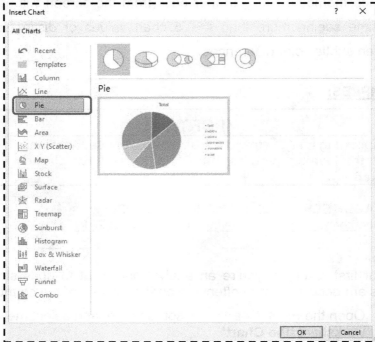

A chart similar to the below should now be displayed:

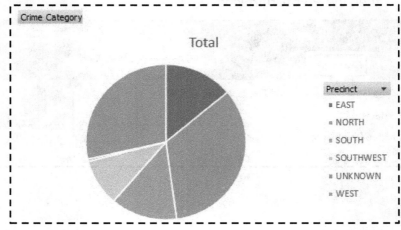

5. From the Ribbon select **PivotChart Tools : Design**, then the **'Quick Layout'** drop-down arrow

6. Select the <u>first option</u> from the **'Quick Layout'** drop-down box

The following Pie Chart should now be displayed:

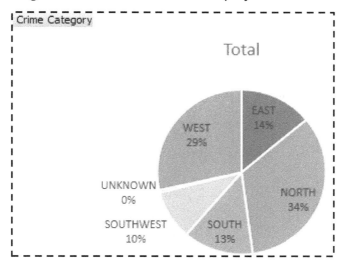

7. Edit the **Chart Title** by double-clicking inside the "Total" field, change text from 'Total' to '**Crimes Reported By Area 02/01/2019 – 03/31/2019**'.

8. *Optional step*: hide the **Field buttons**, right-click over any Field button and select the appropriate hide option

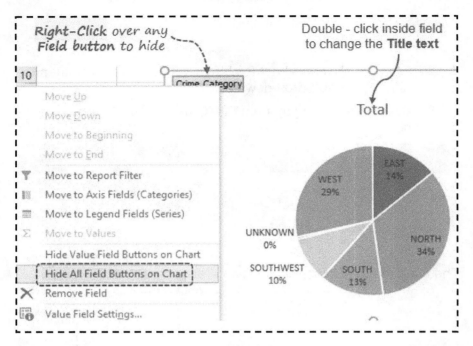

This Pie Chart shows most of the crimes are being committed in the North and West areas of the county.

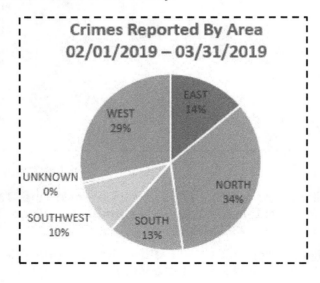

BAR CHART EXAMPLE

Now that we know *where* the majority of crimes are occurring, let's take a look at *what* type of offenses are being reported the most.

1. Open the Pivot_Charts.xlsx spreadsheet and select the **'Bar Chart'** worksheet

2. From the Ribbon select **PivotTable Tools : Analyze** and then the **PivotChart** icon

3. Select the **'Bar'** option

4. Click the **'OK'** button

5. **Move** the chart below the PivotTable report summary

6. **Expand** the **length & width** to allow for easier viewing

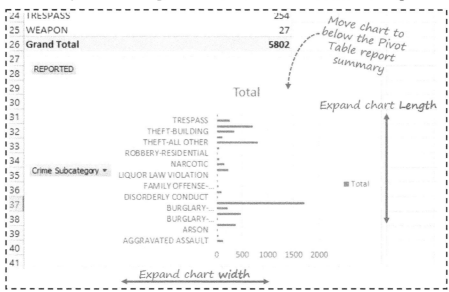

Note: the crime offense **rows** in the bar chart are in descending order. Our display would be more effective and easier to read if we show the crime count total reported in cascading order.

7. Place your cursor in cell **'A1'** and click the drop-down arrow

8. Select **'More Sort Options…'**

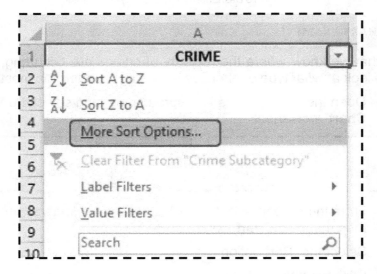

The following dialogue box will appear:

9. Select the **'Ascending (A to Z) by:'** radio button
10. Select **'REPORTED'** from the drop-down box
11. Click the **'OK'** button

With the bar chart in cascading order, we can now easily see 'Car Prowl' is the most often reported crime by a wide margin.

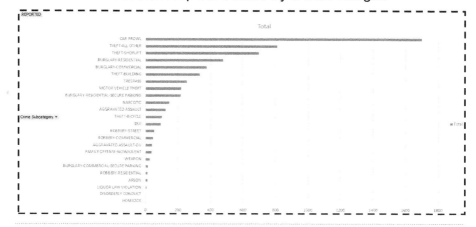

VALUE FILTERS & PIVOTCHARTS

Let's see if we can focus our resources on the **TOP 5** crimes reported.

12. Place your cursor in cell **'A1'** and click the drop-down arrow

13. Select **'Value Filters'** then **'Top 10...'**

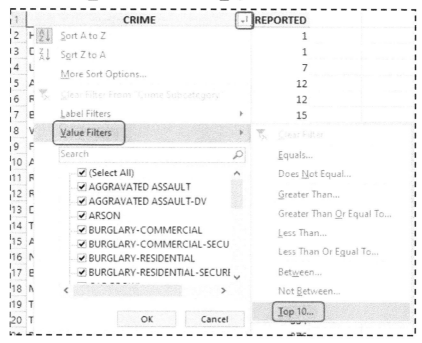

The following dialogue box will appear:

14. Change the quantity to **5** and click the '**OK**' button

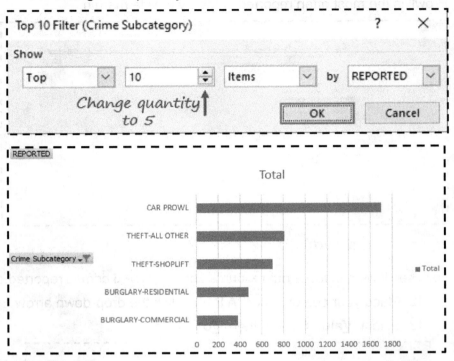

CHART STYLES

Next, let's improve the readability of the chart.

15. With the chart *active*, from the Ribbon select **PivotChart Tools : Design**

16. Under '**Chart Styles**' select the third option

STACKED BAR CHART

Lastly, let's see if we can gain more insight into *where* these **TOP 5** crimes are being reported by using a <u>stacked</u> bar chart.

17. With the chart *active*, from the **'PivotChart Fields'** pane on the left side of the worksheet drag **'Precinct'** to the **'Legend Series'** box.

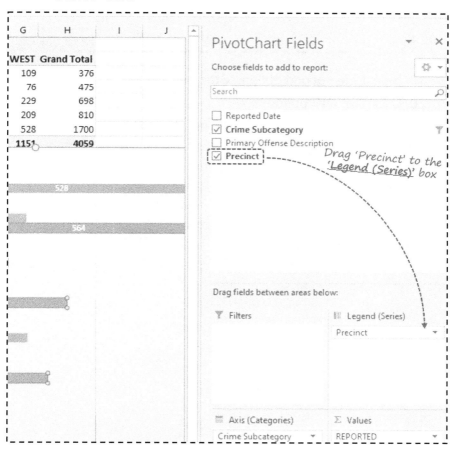

18. From the Ribbon select **PivotChart Tools : Design** then the **Change Chart Type** icon

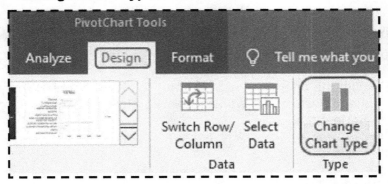

19. Select the second option. **'Stacked Bar'**.

20. Click the **'OK'** button

A stacked bar chart similar to the following should now be displayed:

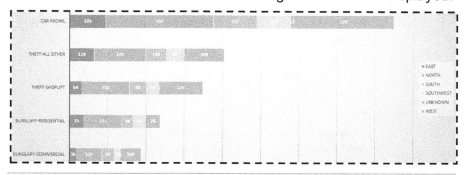

LINE CHART EXAMPLE

The next part of your analysis involves understanding crime trends. Are reported crimes increasing, decreasing, or staying the same?

1. Open the Pivot_Charts.xlsx spreadsheet and select the **'Line Chart'** worksheet

GROUPING PIVOT CHART DATE DATA

You've determined crimes reported **by week** is the best measure. Therefore, you need to take a few additional steps to prepare the data before you can create the Pivot Chart.

2. Select cell **'A2'**, **right click** and then choose the **'Group...'** option

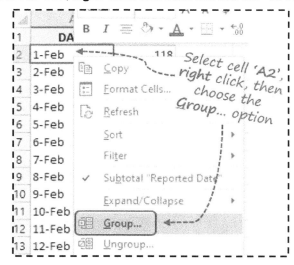

3. Complete the following grouping:
  - Uncheck the **'Starting at:'** and **'Ending at:'** boxes
  - Change the date values to **start on a Sunday (2/3/2019)** and **end on a Saturday (3/30/2019)**. *In a real world situation, this would require looking at a calendar*
  - For the **'By'** box select only **'Days'**
  - Change the **'Number of days:'** quantity to **7**
  - Click the **'OK'** button

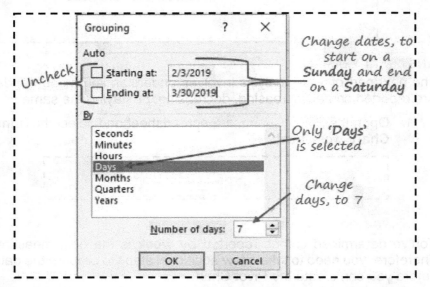

The following count of crimes by week, should now be displayed:

	A	B
1	**DATE** ▼	**CRIMES**
2	<2/3/2019	224
3	2/3/2019 - 2/9/2019	647
4	2/10/2019 - 2/16/2019	676
5	2/17/2019 - 2/23/2019	922
6	2/24/2019 - 3/2/2019	784
7	3/3/2019 - 3/9/2019	601
8	3/10/2019 - 3/16/2019	651
9	3/17/2019 - 3/23/2019	607
10	3/24/2019 - 3/30/2019	619
11	>3/30/2019	71
12	**Grand Total**	**5802**

4. From the Ribbon select **PivotTable Tools : Analyze** and then the **PivotChart** icon

5. Select **'Line'**, then the **'Line with Markers'** option

6. Click the **'OK'** button

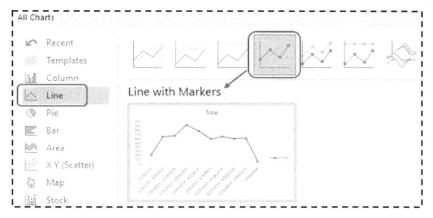

7. **Move** the chart below the PivotTable report summary and **Expand** the **length & width** to allow for easier viewing

Let's improve the readability by hiding the partial weeks of data.

8. Click the drop-down arrow for **DATE (**cell **'A1')** and **uncheck**:
   - <2/3/2019
   - >3/30/2019

9. Click the **'OK'** button

10. With the chart *active*, from the Ribbon select **PivotChart Tools : Design**

11. Under **'Chart Styles'** select the second option

12. Change the title to '**Crimes Reported By Week 02/03/2019 - 03/30/2019**'

A chart similar to below should now be displayed.

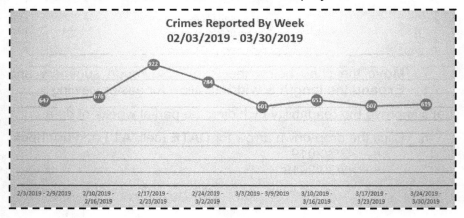

This chart shows a spike in crime in the last two weeks in February. Further investigation into the reasons why may now be explored.

COLUMN CHART EXAMPLE

Based on previous analysis, we know Car Prowls are the most frequently reported crime. Let's see if this offense is the largest contributing factor to the spike in overall crime for the last two weeks in February.

1. Open the Pivot_Charts.xlsx spreadsheet and select the
    'Column Chart' worksheet

POSITIVE & NEGATIVE VALUES WHEN CHARTING

We want to analyze the data for only Car Prowls **by week**. We'll be
measuring the difference as a percent from the previous week.
Before creating the Pivot Chart, we'll first create this metric.

2. Select cell **'B4'**, **right-click**, and **select**:
    - Show Value As
    - % Difference From…

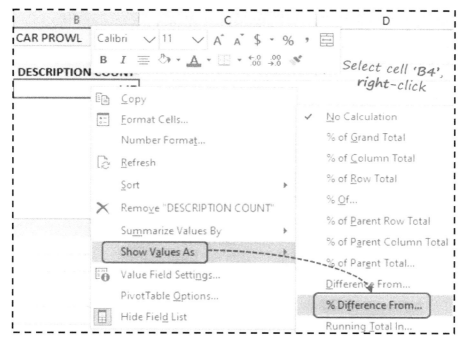

3. When prompted, click the drop-down arrow for **'Base Item:'**
    and select **(previous)**

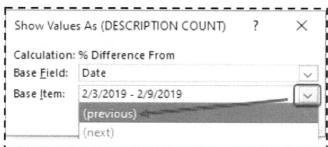

4. Click the **'OK'** button

5. From the Ribbon select **PivotTable Tools : Analyze** and then the **PivotChart** icon

6. Select **'Column'**, then the option **'Clustered Column'**

7. Click the **'OK'** button

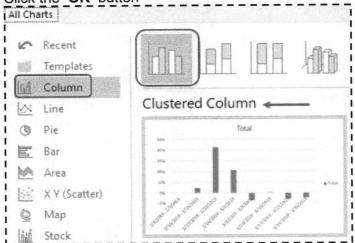

8. **Move** the chart below the PivotTable report summary and **Expand** the **length & width** to allow for easier viewing

9. Hide the **Field buttons, right-click over any Field button** and select **'Hide All Field Buttons on Chart'**

10. With the chart *active*, from the Ribbon select **PivotChart Tools : Design**

11. From the **'Quick Layout'** drop-down box select the <u>fifth option</u>

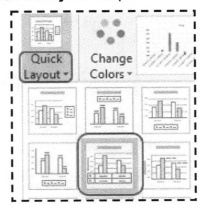

12. Under **'Chart Styles'**, select a dark background option

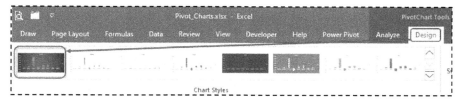

13. With the chart *active* Click the **✚** (plus) symbol and **uncheck 'Axis Titles'**

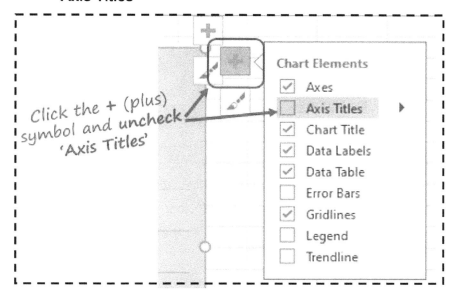

Click the + (plus) symbol and uncheck 'Axis Titles'

14. Change the title to '**% Increase or Decrease of Car Prowls By Week 02/10/2019 - 03/30/2019**'

A chart *similar* to below should now be displayed:

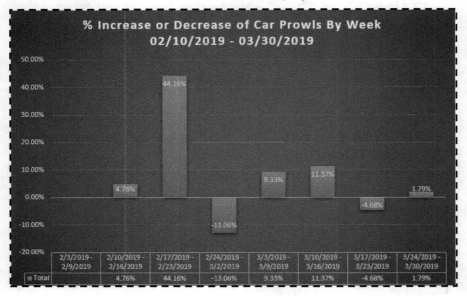

As we can see from this bar chart, the data shows some correlation between Car Prowls and the spike in overall crime for the week of 02/17/2019 – 02/23/2019. However, further investigation is needed to understand the contributing factors to the spike in crime the last week in February.

CHAPTER 9

In the previous chapters, we focused on *summary level* analysis. PivotTables also give us the capability to analyze individual results for comparisons, such as ranking and sorting our results. This may be accomplished without the need to manually sort or add additional calculated columns to our original data source.

EXAMPLE:
In this chapter we'll demonstrate how to:

- Rank each Sales Person by their individual *Total* & *Average Sales*

WEB ADDRESS & FILE NAME FOR EXERCISE:
https://bentonbooks.wixsite.com/bentonbooks/excel-2019
FruitSales.xlsx

Sample data for this chapter, due to space limitations **the entire data set is not displayed**.

	A	B	C	D	E	F	G	H	I
1	REGION	SALES PERSON FIRST NAME	SALES PERSON LAST NAME	SALES PERSON ID	QUARTER	APPLES	ORANGES	MANGOS	TOTAL
2	Central	Bob	Taylor	1174	1	1,810	2,039	1,771	5,620
3	Central	Helen	Smith	833	1	102	354	59	516
4	Central	Jill	Johnson	200	1	93	322	54	469
5	Central	Sally	Morton	500	1	595	824	556	1,975
6	Central	Sam	Becker	800	1	863	1,092	824	2,779
7	East	Abbey	Williams	690	1	346	237	260	843
8	East	John	Dower	255	1	260	178	195	633
9	East	John	Wilson	300	1	286	196	215	696
10	East	Mary	Nelson	600	1	315	215	236	766
11	East	Sarah	Taylor	900	1	381	261	285	927
12	West	Alex	Steller	1000	1	163	212	127	502
13	West	Billy	Winchester	1156	1	179	234	140	552
14	West	Helen	Simpson	817	1	148	193	116	457
15	West	Jack	Smith	100	1	111	145	87	343
16	West	Joe	Tanner	400	1	122	160	96	377
17	West	Peter	Graham	700	1	134	175	105	415
18	Central	Bob	Taylor	1174	2	113	390	65	567
19	Central	Helen	Smith	833	2	1,006	1,393	940	3,338
64	West	Joe	Tanner	400	4	2,833	2,886	2,796	8,516
65	West	Peter	Graham	700	4	4,392	4,473	4,334	13,199

Create a new PivotTable report, to see screenshot illustrations of steps #1 - #3, please see chapter 4 Basic PivotTable Functionality, page 12:

1. Open the FruitSales.xlsx spreadsheet and select **cells 'A1:I65'**
2. From the Ribbon select **Insert : PivotTable**
3. Click the '**OK**' button

A new tab will be created and the *'PivotTable Fields' pane* should appear on the left side of your screen.

4. In the *'PivotTable Fields' pane* **drag** the following fields:
    - **SALES PERSON ID** *(Rows section)*
    - **TOTAL _three_** times *(∑ Values section)*

A report *similar* to the following should be displayed.

*Note: all three of the '**Sum of TOTAL**' columns are currently the same. We will be addressing this in the ensuing steps.*

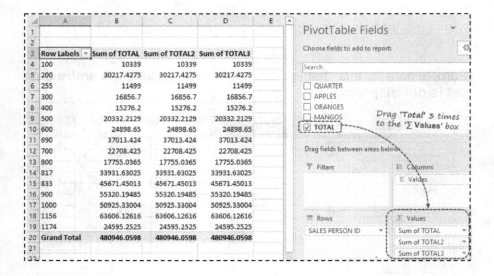

5. Change the label text for the following cells:
    - 'A3' to **'SALES PERSON ID'**
    - 'B3' to **'TOTAL SALES'**
    - 'C3' to **'AVERAGE SALES'**
    - 'D3' to **'RANK'**

6. Change the formatting for columns **'B'** & **'C'** to a **currency** of your choice with _zero decimal places_. In this example I will use the British Pound.

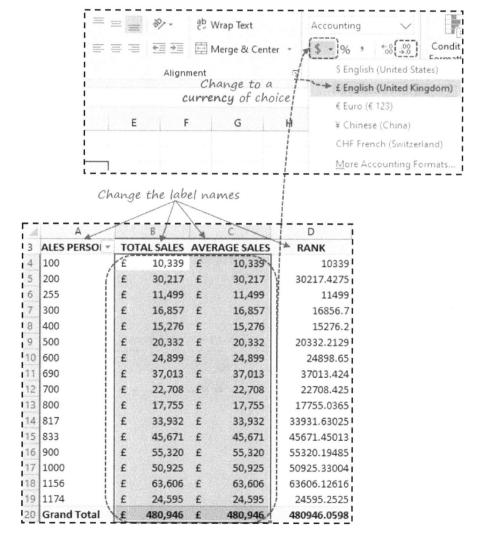

7. In the *'PivotTable Fields' pane*, in the **'∑ Values'** section, click the drop-down arrow for **'AVERAGE SALES'**

8. From the sub-menu select the **'Value Field Settings...'** option

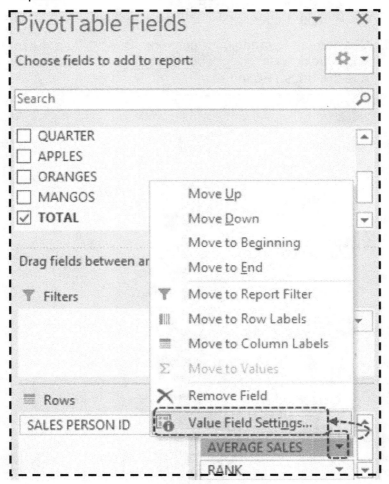

The following dialogue box should appear

9. From the '**Summarize Values By**' list select '**Average**'.
*Note: this will change the '**Custom Name:**' to '**Average of TOTAL'**, change back to '**AVERAGE SALES**'*

10. Click the '**OK**' button

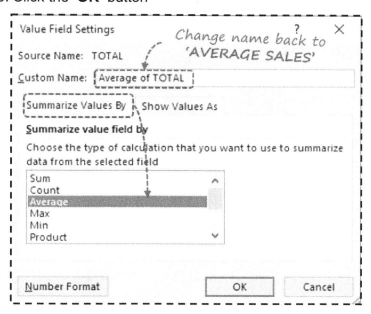

11. In the *'PivotTable Fields' pane*, in the '∑ *Values*' section, click the drop-down arrow for '**RANK**'

12. From the sub- menu select the '**Value Field Settings…**' option

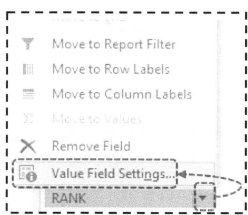

13. From the **Value Field Settings** dialogue box:
- Select the tab **'Show Values As'**
- From the '**Show values as**' drop-down list select **'Rank Largest to Smallest'**
- For the **'Base field:'** box select **'SALES PERSON ID'**
- Click the **'OK'** button

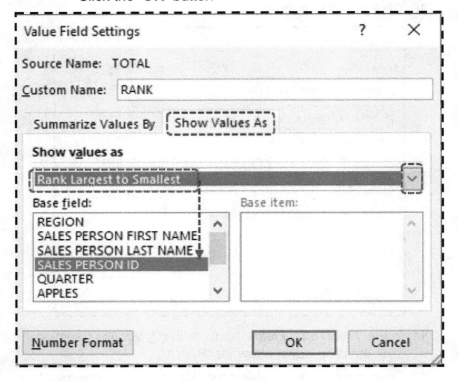

*The results should look **similar** to the following:*

	A	B	C	D
3	SALES PERSON ID ▾	TOTAL SALES	AVERAGE SALES	RANK
4	100	£ 10,339	£ 2,585	16
5	200	£ 30,217	£ 7,554	7
6	255	£ 11,499	£ 2,875	15
7	300	£ 16,857	£ 4,214	13
8	400	£ 15,276	£ 3,819	14
9	500	£ 20,332	£ 5,083	11
10	600	£ 24,899	£ 6,225	8
11	690	£ 37,013	£ 9,253	5
12	700	£ 22,708	£ 5,677	10
13	800	£ 17,755	£ 4,439	12
14	817	£ 33,932	£ 8,483	6
15	833	£ 45,671	£ 11,418	4
16	900	£ 55,320	£ 13,830	2
17	1000	£ 50,925	£ 12,731	3
18	1156	£ 63,606	£ 15,902	1
19	1174	£ 24,595	£ 6,149	9
20	**Grand Total**	£ 480,946	£ 7,515	

Let's improve the readability:

14. Select cell **'A3'** and from the **PivotTable Tools** Ribbon select the **'Design'** tab

15. Check the box **'Banded Rows'**

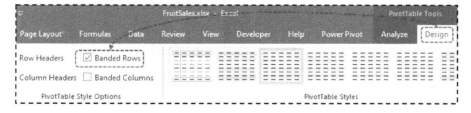

16. Place your cursor in cell **'A3'** and click the drop-down arrow

17. Select the option called **'More Sort Options…'**

The following dialogue box will appear:

18. Select the **'Descending (Z to A) by:'** radio button

19. Select **'RANK'** from the drop-down box

20. Click the **'OK'** button

We now have a nicely formatted report that shows us each Sales Person's *sales rank* and their Total and Average Sales.

	A	B	C	D
3	SALES PERSON ID ⤓	TOTAL SALES	AVERAGE SALES	RANK
4	1156	£ 63,606	£ 15,902	1
5	900	£ 55,320	£ 13,830	2
6	1000	£ 50,925	£ 12,731	3
7	833	£ 45,671	£ 11,418	4
8	690	£ 37,013	£ 9,253	5
9	817	£ 33,932	£ 8,483	6
10	200	£ 30,217	£ 7,554	7
11	600	£ 24,899	£ 6,225	8
12	1174	£ 24,595	£ 6,149	9
13	700	£ 22,708	£ 5,677	10
14	500	£ 20,332	£ 5,083	11
15	800	£ 17,755	£ 4,439	12
16	300	£ 16,857	£ 4,214	13
17	400	£ 15,276	£ 3,819	14
18	255	£ 11,499	£ 2,875	15
19	100	£ 10,339	£ 2,585	16
20	Grand Total	£ 480,946	£ 7,515	

CHAPTER 10

PIVOTTABLES FROM IMPORTED FILES & THE EXCEL® DATA MODEL

Like with many tasks in Excel®, file importing and parsing can be accomplished in multiple ways. The following example describes how to read and parse a **.CSV** (comma separated value) file using Excel's® Data Model. After the data is imported, we'll create two PivotTable reports.

THE EXCEL® DATA MODEL

The Excel® Data Model is a feature in which data from different sources can be brought together into a single workbook via a computer or network connection and queries. Once this information is in the workbook, you'll be able to create PivotTables and Charts.

This type of reporting may also be achieved by using macros (Visual Basic for Applications), Power Pivot, Power Query *(please see next chapter)*, and Power View. Deciding which method to use depends on a variety of factors, such as:

- The amount of data you're analyzing
- The complexity and time it takes to complete your analysis
- Your audience's requirements
- Your skill level with Excel® and the version you're using

In the following example, the reporting is straightforward. We'll be reporting on less than 100 records and our Excel® Data Model will contain only one data source (a .CSV file).

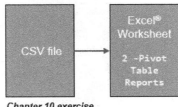

Chapter 10 exercise

Chapter 11 describes how to consolidate data with larger record counts and from multiple workbooks to create a PivotTable using **'Power Query'**.

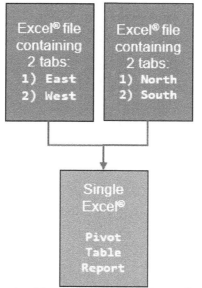

Chapter 11 exercise – using Power Query

EXAMPLE:

You're a Business Analyst and a request has been made to change a monthly employee sales report. Management would now like:

- A Regional sales summary by month
- Employee sales grouped and subtotaled by Region

Employee sales are captured in a legacy system. This older system produces a monthly *.CSV file* and saves it to a location on a company server. To save yourself time formatting the same report each month you create two PivotTables to import and format the data.

WEB ADDRESS & FILE NAMES FOR EXERCISE:
https://bentonbooks.wixsite.com/bentonbooks/excel-2019
EmployeeSales.csv
MonthlySalesReport.xlsx

From .CSV file:

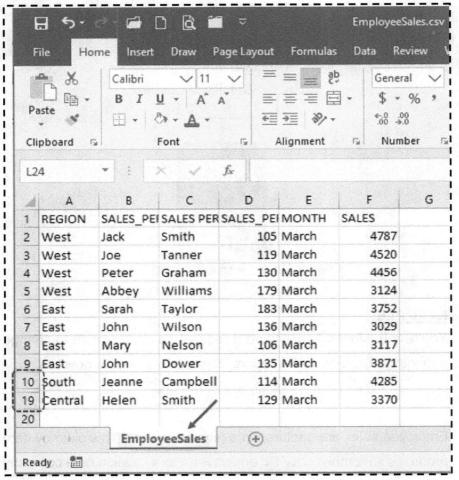

To Excel® Report:

	A	B	C	D	E	F
1	Monthly Employee & Region Sales Report					
2						
3	**REGION**	**MONTH** ▾			**SALES**	**MONTH** ▾
4	**EMPLOYEE** ▾	March			**REGION** ▾	March
5	⊟ Central				Central	£19,054
6	Becker	£4,647			East	£13,769
7	Johnson	£4,386			South	£20,979
8	Morton	£3,425			West	£16,887
9	Smith	£3,370			**TOTAL**	**£70,689**
10	Taylor	£3,226				
11	**Central Total**	**£19,054**				
12	⊟ East					
13	Dower	£3,871				
14	Nelson	£3,117				
15	Taylor	£3,752				
16	Wilson	£3,029				
17	**East Total**	**£13,769**				
18	⊟ South					
19	Bates	£3,834				
20	Blatchford	£4,350				
21	Campbell	£4,285				
22	Lewis	£4,805				
23	Tansae	£3,705				
24	**South Total**	**£20,979**				
25	⊟ West					
26	Graham	£4,456				
27	Smith	£4,787				
28	Tanner	£4,520				
29	Williams	£3,124				
30	**West Total**	**£16,887**				
31	**TOTAL**	**£70,689**				

IMPORTANT!
The following steps & screenshots use **Excel® version 2019**, the interface for the previous versions of **Excel®** is very different.

1. Download the EmployeeSales.csv exercise file to a location you can easily access such as a temporary folder or your desktop

2. Open the MonthlySalesReport.xlsx spreadsheet

3. From the Ribbon select **Data** and then **'From Text/CSV'**

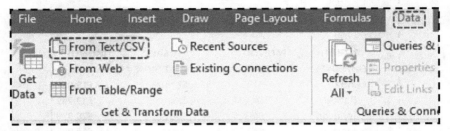

4. Open the location where the EmployeeSales.**csv** file is located

5. **Select the file** and click the **'Import'** button

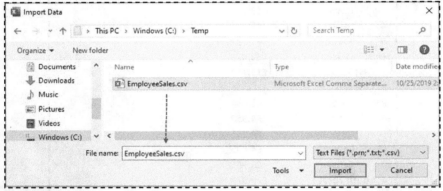

The following prompt will appear:

6. Click the **'Load'** drop-down box and select the **'Load To...'** option

7. For the **'Import Data'** prompt:
   - Select the radio button for **'PivotTable Report'**
   - Select the radio button for **'Existing worksheet'** enter **=$E$3** for the cell location
   - Click the check box for **'Add this data to the Data Model'**
   - Click the **'OK'** button

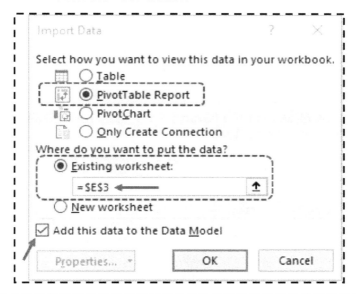

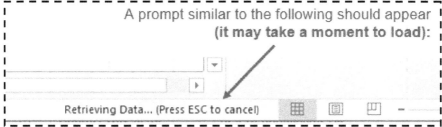

8. In the *'PivotTable Fields' pane* select the following fields:
   - REGION *(Rows section)*
   - MONTH *(Columns section)*
   - SALES *(Σ Values section)*

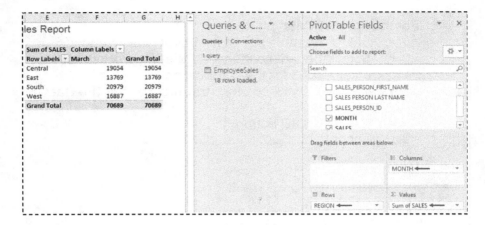

9. **Right-click** over the **'Grand Total'** field **(cell 'G4')** and select **'Remove Grand Total'**

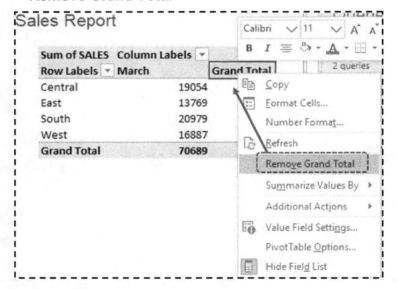

10. Formatting changes:
   - Cell **'E3'** text to **'SALES'**
   - Cell **'F3'** text to **'MONTH'**
   - Cell **'E4'** text to **'REGION'**
   - Cell **'E9'** text to **'TOTAL'**
   - Cells **'F5:F9'** currency format of your preference

▲	A	B	C	D	E	F
1	Monthly Employee & Region Sales Report					
2						
3					SALES	MONTH ▾
4					REGION ▾	March
5					Central	£19,054
6					East	£13,769
7					South	£20,979
8					West	£16,887
9					TOTAL	£70,689

Copy the PivotTable

11. Select cells **'E3:F9'** right-click and select **'Copy'** or press **Ctrl+C** on your keyboard

12. Place your cursor in cell **'A3'** and press **Ctrl+V** (paste) on your keyboard

13. Inside the *'PivotTable Fields' pane* select the **'SALES PERSON LAST NAME'** box

14. Place your cursor in cell **'A5' right-click** and select **'Subtotal "REGION"**

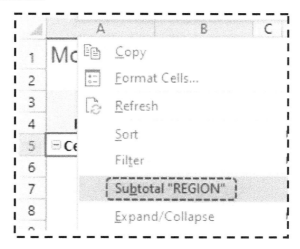

15. Formatting changes:
    - Cell **'A3'** text to **'REGION'**
    - Cell **'A4'** text to **'EMPLOYEE'**

The final report should look similar to the following:

	A	B	C	D	E	F
1	Monthly Employee & Region Sales Report					
2						
3	REGION	MONTH ▾			SALES	MONTH ▾
4	EMPLOYEE ▾	March			REGION ▾	March
5	⊟Central				Central	£19,054
6	Becker	£4,647			East	£13,769
7	Johnson	£4,386			South	£20,979
8	Morton	£3,425			West	£16,887
9	Smith	£3,370			TOTAL	£70,689
10	Taylor	£3,226				
11	Central Total	£19,054				
12	⊟East					
13	Dower	£3,871				
14	Nelson	£3,117				
15	Taylor	£3,752				
16	Wilson	£3,029				
17	East Total	£13,769				
18	⊟South					
19	Bates	£3,834				
20	Blatchford	£4,350				
21	Campbell	£4,285				
22	Lewis	£4,805				
23	Tansae	£3,705				
24	South Total	£20,979				
25	⊟West					
26	Graham	£4,456				
27	Smith	£4,787				
28	Tanner	£4,520				
29	Williams	£3,124				
30	West Total	£16,887				
31	TOTAL	£70,689				

Please see Chapter 15 page 160 to learn more about Refreshing PivotTable Data.

CHAPTER 11

CONSOLIDATING DATA FROM SEPARATE WORKBOOKS TO CREATE A SINGLE PIVOTTABLE

A common real-world challenge is collecting data from different sources and assimilating it into a single file where further analysis may be performed. This process is time consuming and prone to errors. As we saw in chapter 10, Microsoft Excel® offers several options to import data. In this chapter, we're going explore how to use another one them called Power Query.

POWER QUERY

Power Query is an extremely useful feature available in newer versions of Excel® [1] that allows users to connect and bring together data from many different sources. Once the information is collected in the Power Query Editor[2] it can be merged or appended. The analysis options are similar to writing your own SQL (**S**tructured **Q**uery **L**anguage) queries, such as grouping, date, text, numeric and

---

[1]*Excel for Office 365, Excel 2019, Excel 2016, Excel 2013, Excel 2010, retrieved 18 November 2019 from Microsoft®*
   https://support.office.com/en-us/article/introduction-to-microsoft-power-query-for-excel-6e92e2f4-2079-4e1f-bad5-89f6269cd605

[2] Power Query for Excel® add-in *, retrieved 18 November 2019 from Microsoft®*
   https://www.microsoft.com/en-us/download/details.aspx?id=39379&CorrelationId=cf9e02f4-a5ed-47fe-b9b9-0bdad0fef6b4

more, all available in an easy-to-use interface.

These queries and their results can be saved and/or loaded into an Excel® spreadsheet, PivotTable, or PivotChart. The data may be refreshed for up-to-date reporting or testing without having to make any changes to your original work.

Power Query can also be useful for development projects such as temporary or project based reporting or prototyping to assist in refining your customer's data requirements.

Power Query can help you become more efficient and once you start using it, you'll likely find so many ways of incorporating it into your daily work. However, by providing an almost effortless method to merge data, Power Query brings with it a high risk of inaccurate analysis and reporting. There is no substitute for understanding your underlying content, how it is structured, and the quality of the data. Also, having some basic knowledge of data modeling and the relationship between the different data sources is essential.

IMPORTANT!
The following steps & screenshots use **Excel® version 2019**, the interface for the previous versions of **Excel®** is very different.

EXAMPLE:

You've been asked to *consolidate* separate monthly Regional sales plans for 2020 from four regions into a single high level summary.

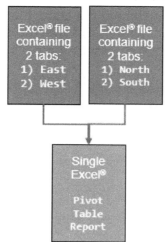

WEB ADDRESS & FILE NAME FOR EXERCISE:
https://bentonbooks.wixsite.com/bentonbooks/excel-2019
1. Data_File - East_West.xlsx
2. Data_File - North_South.xlsx

ADDITIONAL STEP FOR THIS CHAPTER

Save the **Data_File - East_West.xlsx** and **Data_File - North_South.xlsx** files to a location you can easily access such as a temporary folder or your desktop.

1. Create a new blank Excel® spreadsheet, by pressing **(CTRL + N)** on your keyboard

2. From the Ribbon select **Data**

3. Click the **'Get Data'** drop-down arrow and select **From File** : **From Workbook**

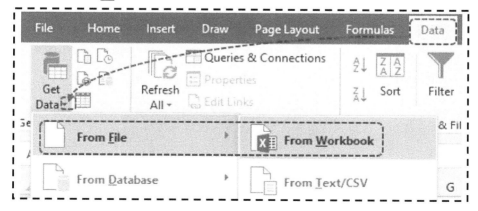

4. Open the location where the **Data_File - East_West.xlsx** file is located, **select it**, and click the **'Import'** button

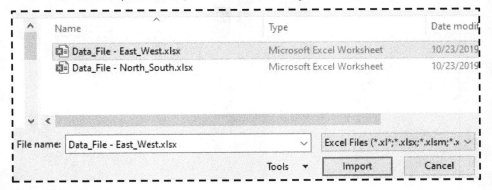

The following prompt will appear:

5. Complete the following:
   - Click the check box for **'Select multiple items'**
   - Click the check box for **'East'**
   - Click the check box for **'West'**
   - Click the **'Load'** drop-down arrow and select the **'Load To...'** option

6. For the **'Import Data'** prompt:
    - Select the radio button for **'Only Create Connection'**
    - Click the check box for **'Add this data to the Data Model'**
    - Click the **'OK'** button

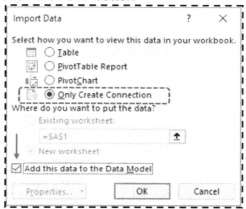

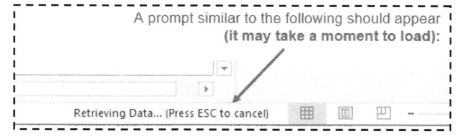

When the connection is established, your screen should look similar to the following:

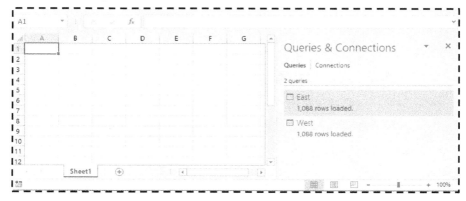

7. Repeat **steps 3 – 6** for the file **Data_File - North_South.xlsx**

After the connection to the file **Data_File - North_South.xlsx** has been established, we'll *combine the queries*. Once this is done, we can create our consolidated PivotTable report.

Essentially, what we've completed so far is create two connections that *select all* data from the two separate workbooks. Next, we need to bring these two queries together by creating a new query. There are two options for joining queries '**Append**' and '**Merge**':

APPEND VS. MERGE IN POWER QUERY

Append: is used when the data you're joining is structurally similar (i.e. the same number of columns and column names) and you want to combine *all the rows* from each query together.

Think of this like copying all the data from one file and pasting it to the bottom of another to create one large file with all the records.

Merge: is utilized when the data you're joining contains *only select columns in common*. These *common columns* may have different column names, but the content and data type between them is the same.

In this situation, we have a primary query and *primary key value*, this key value matches an identical value in a secondary query. The result of the new query brings together only those records in which the key values match between the two queries.

Unlike **appending** where we're bringing together *all* of the data, when **merging** we're only combining *select* columns and rows from the different sources.

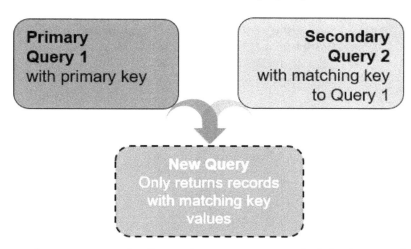

In our example the column names and data types of the content are the same, and we want <u>all the rows from each query</u> for our report, therefore we'll be using the **'Append'** method.

8. From the Ribbon select **Data**

9. Click the **'Get Data'** drop-down arrow and select **Combine Queries : Append**

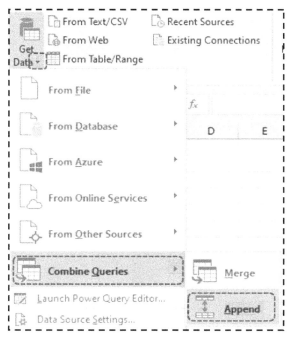

10. Select the following when prompted:
   - Select the radio button for **'Three or more tables'**
   - Select all *4 tables* and click the **'Add >>'** button
   - Click the **'OK'** button

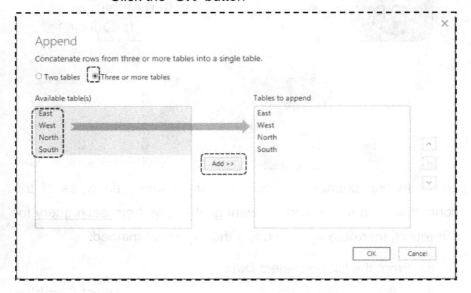

This will open the Power Query Editor

11. Select the '**Close & Load**' drop-down arrow and then '**Close & Load To..**'

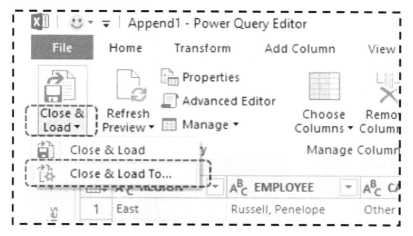

It may take a moment for the following prompt to appear:

12. For the '**Import Data**' prompt:
   - Select the radio button for '**PivotTable Report**'
   - Click the check box for '**Add this data to the Data Model**'
   - Click the '**OK**' button

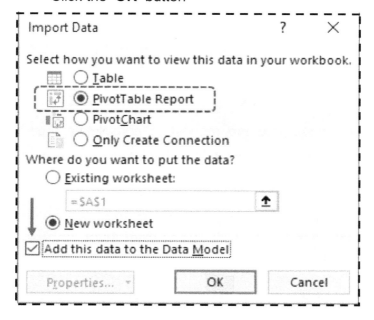

We've taken four separate queries and combined them into one and now may create and modify the PivotTable as needed.

13. In the *'PivotTable Fields' pane* select the following fields:
- REGION *(Rows section)*
- PLAN   *(∑ Values section)*

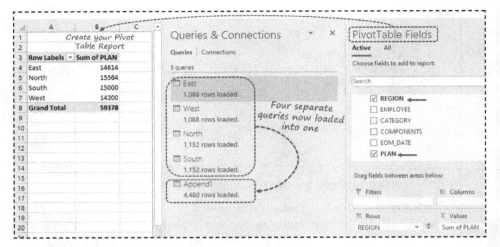

14. Optionally, format the PivotTable report to improve readability

REGION ⏷	2020 PLANS
East	$ 14,614
North	$ 15,564
South	$ 15,000
West	$ 14,200
TOTAL	$ 59,378

We've now completed the request to consolidate four Regional detailed monthly sales plans for the year 2020 into a single high level summary.

Please see *Chapter 15 page 160* *to learn more about Refreshing PivotTable Data.*

CHAPTER 12

WHAT IS A DASHBOARD?

A *business* or *digital* dashboard in the simplest terms, is a display of metrics in numeric or graphical form. These metrics or what is commonly referred to as *measures*, range widely depending on the customer and type of organization.

The components of a dashboard vary, but typically include one-or-more of the following, *at a glance*:

- Provide an answer to a business question
- Show comparisons such as this year's (TY) sales compared to last year's (LY) sales
- The progress or status of meeting a target, for example reaching a sales, production, or safety goal
- Trends such as identifying if an activity is trending up, down, or about the same

A dashboard is usually limited to one functional area, like Manufacturing, Human Resources, Finance, Logistics, or Marketing and may be static or interactive.

DASHBOARD DESIGN

The elements of a well-designed digital dashboard include working closing with the consumers of the dashboard to understand:

- ✓ How are they planning to use the information in the dashboard to improve their objectives? Will they be tracking performance, monitoring progress, or something else?

✓ How will they measure the success or usefulness of the dashboard?

✓ Does your audience require separate slices of the data? Perhaps a manger is interested in seeing only their own geographic area.

✓ How will your audience view or access the dashboard? In paper form, on a website, mobile device? You'll want to be mindful of spacing and the use of colors if your audience reads the dashboard on paper printed in black and white ink. Likewise, you may need to limit the amount of information displayed or use of charts if viewing on a mobile device.

✓ Will the dashboard be temporary or a permanent part of your customer's daily, weekly, or monthly routine?

✓ What data sources and at what *frequency* (real-time, daily, weekly, or monthly) are available for your dashboard?

✓ Are there data restrictions or information security concerns with publishing the dashboard?

✓ How will you maintain the dashboard? Will it require manual updating or will your design allow the data to be refreshed when a customer accesses it? *This may also be dependent on the required permissions to the data source.*

The purpose of the dashboard should be clear to anyone viewing it and include:

- A *title* or brief description of the dashboard
- The *time period* the data covers

It's been my experience to start small when creating a dashboard. Once your customers start using the information, they almost always ask for more and request changes to the layout.

You'll want to manage customer expectations accordingly. What seems like a simple change or graphic to your customer may require a lot of data preparation behind the scenes. It is important to balance the amount of time you spend creating and maintaining the dashboard with the benefits it provides.

DASHBOARD GRAPHICS

In addition to charts, Excel® offers a number of built-in graphics to aid in dashboard development. In the following chapters we'll examine how to use some of these, along with creating a multi-PivotTable based dashboard.

In chapter 8, we explored how to use four types of **Pivot Charts**. In this chapter, we'll explore **Sparklines**, **Add-Ins**, **Icon Sets**, and two additional Excel® charts (Doughnut & Map).

IMPORTANT!
Not all chart types work with PivotTable data, these include, *'Map'*, *'Funnel'*, *'Scatter'* and more. We can still use these graphs in our dashboards, but the data must be prepared in a way compatible with the particular chart type.

The following describes some of the *most commonly used* illustrative tools in Excel®, however, <u>does not review all</u> visual mechanisms available.

DOUGHNUT CHART

Example of a Doughnut Chart with a Text Box added to display a percentage

A **'Doughnut Chart'** is a variation of a **'Pie Chart'**, it too is most appropriate for illustrating percentages as part of the whole. However, when using in a dashboard typically <u>only two values</u> are compared. This is because Doughnut charts can be difficult to read when more than two or three values are being evaluated.

>DOUGHNUT CHART EXAMPLE

Let's walk through an exercise on how to create a Doughnut chart using PivotTable data.

1. Open the DashboardGraphics.xlsx spreadsheet and select the worksheet **'Doughnut Chart'**

2. From the Ribbon select **PivotTable Tools : Analyze** and then the **PivotChart** icon

IMPORTANT!
If you do not see the **_PivotTable Tools : Analyze_** option on your Ribbon, click any PivotTable cell. This option only appears when a PivotTable field is active.

3. Select **'Pie'** from the dialogue box
4. Select the last option **'Doughnut'**

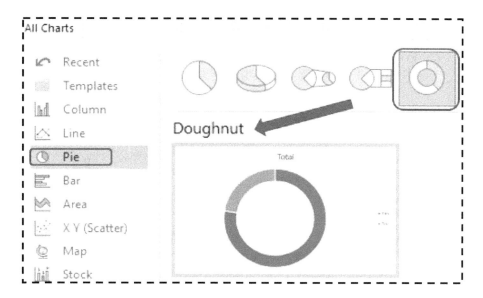

5. Click the **'OK'** button

A chart similar to the below should now be displayed:

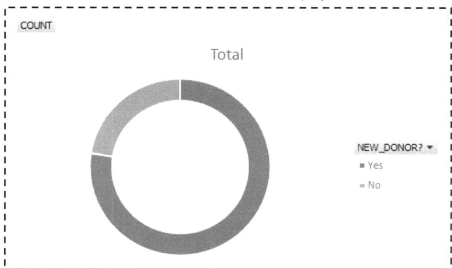

The following steps 6 – 20 are optional

6. Hide the **Field buttons**, right-click over any Field button and select **'Hide All Field Buttons on Chart'**

7. With the chart selected, click the plus **+** button next to the chart and uncheck the **'Legend'** box

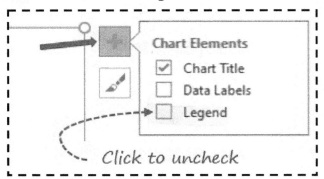

8. Click the **paint brush** button, select **'Color'** then a **'Monochromatic' color** of your choice

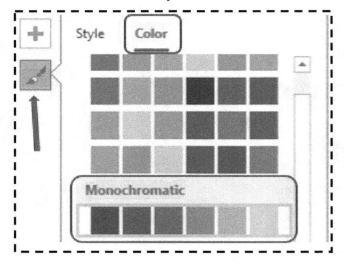

9. **Double click** to select the **smaller** portion of the Doughnut chart

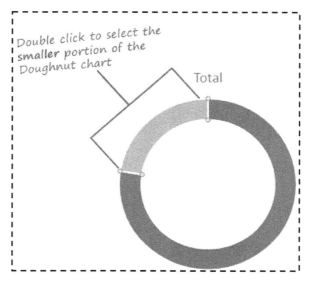

Double click to select the smaller portion of the Doughnut chart

Total

10. From the **'Format Data Point'** menu, select the **'Paint Bucket'** and click the **'Pattern fill'** radio button

11. Select a pattern format of your choice

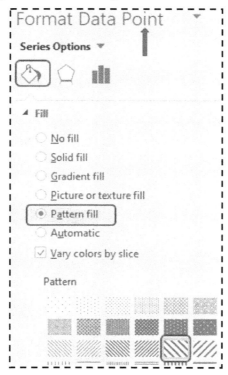

12. Click outside the chart, for example cell **'C2'**

13. From the **'Ribbon'** select '**Insert** : **Illustrations** : **Shapes**'

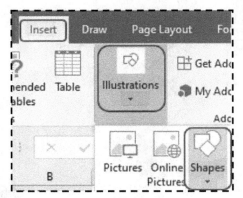

14. From the **'Shapes'** drop-down menu select the **'Text Box'** shape

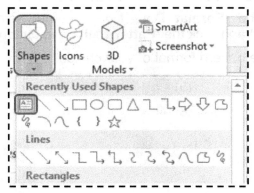

15. Drag the upside-down cross to the center of the Doughnut chart and draw a square

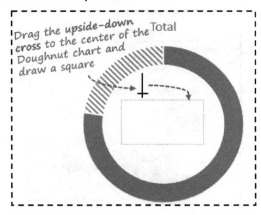

16. With your cursor inside the **TextBox**, select the **formula bar** and enter **=$B$2** *(press the 'Enter' button on your keyboard) to <u>link the formula</u> to the TextBox)*

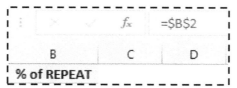

17. Change the <u>**font size**</u> and <u>**style**</u> of the TextBox to a theme of your choice

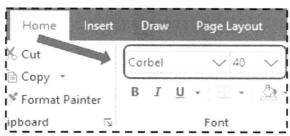

18. Select TextBox and **right-click**, from the sub-menu select **'Format Shape…'**

19. Select the **'Paint Bucket'** and click the **'No Fill'** and **'No Line'** radio buttons

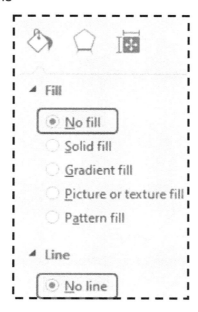

20. Change the <u>title</u> from **'Total'** to **'% of Repeat Donors'**

A chart similar to the below should now be displayed:

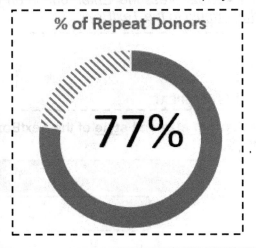

GEOGRAPHIC (MAPS)

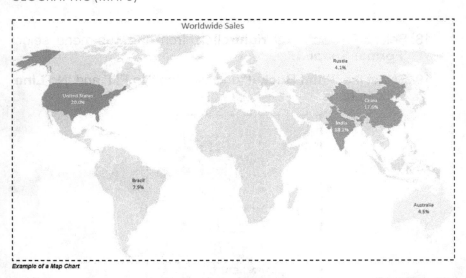

Example of a Map Chart

The **Map** chart type is useful for understanding *high level* geographic information. At the time of this book's publication, the **Map chart** <u>does not support</u> lower level geographical data such as cities. For example, if you were analyzing a percentage of sales by US State, and wanted to drill-down to see sales by city in the State of California, this chart type would not work.

Also, this chart type <u>does not work</u> with PivotTable data and creating or updating the chart <u>requires an internet connection</u>. Existing Map charts do not require a network access.

IMPORTANT!
The following steps & screenshots use **Excel® version 2019**, the interface for the previous versions of **Excel®** is very different.

>MAP EXAMPLE

1. Open the DashboardGraphics.xlsx spreadsheet and select the worksheet **'Map Chart'**

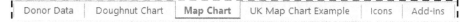

2. Select cells '**A2:B20**'

3. From the Ribbon select **INSERT**

4. Under the **Charts** menu, click the **Maps** drop-down arrow

5. Choose '**Filled Map**'

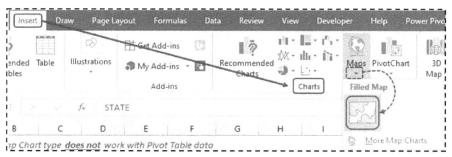

6. With the chart selected, click the plus **+** button next to the chart

7. Select the arrow next to **'Data Labels'** then **'Show More Data Label Options...'**

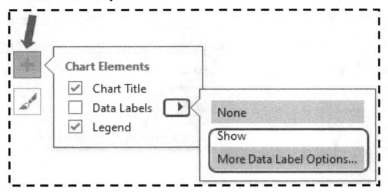

8. From the **'Format Data Labels...'** menu select
   - **Category Name**
   - **Value**
   - **Separator** drop-down choose: **(New Line)**

A chart *similar* to the below should now be displayed:

*You may need to **expand** the **length & width** of the **Map chart** for better viewing*

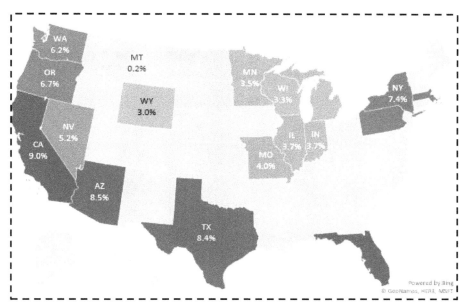

To see a United Kingdom Map Chart example, please click on the worksheet tab labeled '**UK Map Chart Example**'.

ICONS (GRAPHICS)

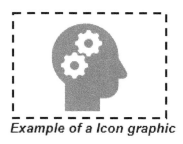

Example of a Icon graphic

Icons are a simple way to give your dashboard visual appeal. There are a variety of options to choose from and their fill-color can be changed to enhance their use.

>ICON EXAMPLE

1. Open the DashboardGraphics.xlsx spreadsheet and select the worksheet '**Icons**'

2. From the Ribbon select **INSERT**

3. Click the **Illustrations** drop-down arrow then **Icons**

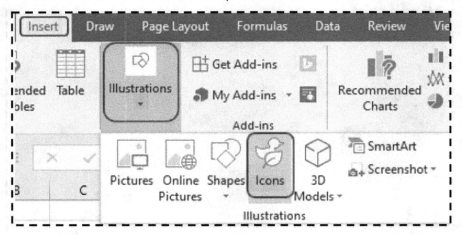

4. When prompted, under the **'Analytics'** section, **select the up & down arrow chart icons**

5. Click the **'Insert'** button

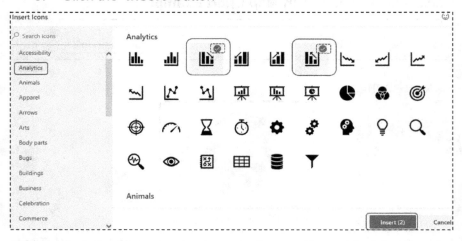

The icons should now be inserted into the worksheet, however they **may be overlapping** each other and need to be separated.

6. Select the **down-arrow graph icon**, **right-click**, and select the option **'Format Graphic'**

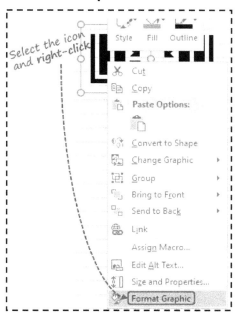

7. When prompted select the **'Fill'** color **red**

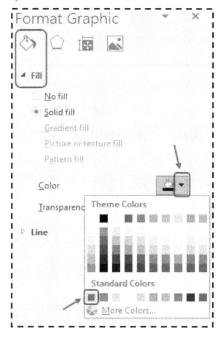

8. **Repeat steps 6 & 7** for the **up-arrow graph icon**, this time select the **'Fill'** color **green**

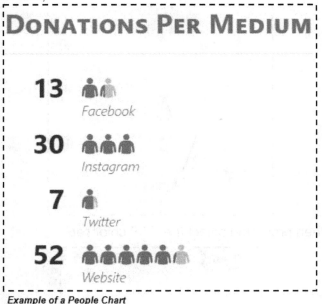

Example of a People Chart

The People Graph is a visually appealing chart type to display numeric amounts versus using a bar or column chart.

The People Graph is considered an **Excel® Add-in**, requiring the user to install before the display will work.

>PEOPLE GRAPH EXAMPLE

1. Open the DashboardGraphics.xlsx spreadsheet and select the worksheet **'Add-in'**
2. From the Ribbon select **INSERT**
3. Click the **People** icon from the **'Add-ins'** section

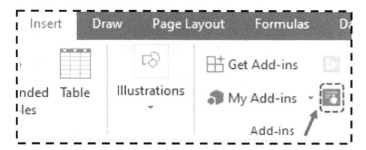

The following prompt should now be displayed:

4.   Click the **'Trust this add-in'** button, it make a minute or two for the add-in to load

5.   After the add-in has loaded select the **'Data'** button

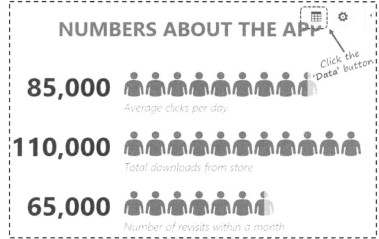

6.   Change the **Title** to **'Amount Raised By Volunteer'**

7. Click the **'Select your data'** button

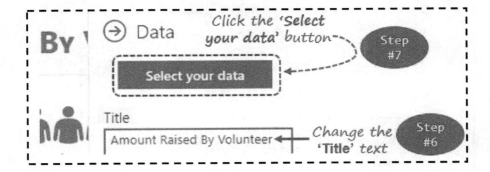

8. Select rows **'A2:B11'** and click the **'Create'** button

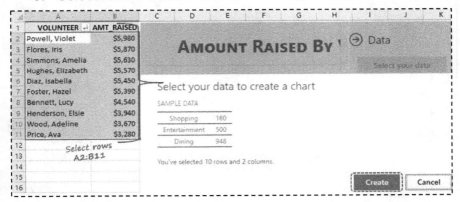

9. Click the **'Settings'** button

10. Select **'Shape'** then the **money bag** symbol

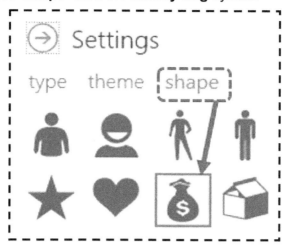

A chart *similar* to the below should now be displayed:

AMOUNT RAISED BY VOLUNTEER

$5,980   💰💰💰💰💰
Powell, Violet

$5,870   💰💰💰💰💰
Flores, Iris

$5,630   💰💰💰💰💰
Simmons, Amelia

$5,570   💰💰💰💰💰
Hughes, Elizabeth

$5,450   💰💰💰💰💰
Diaz, Isabella

SPARKLINES

Sparklines are mini *trend charts* contained inside a single cell of a worksheet. Each sparkline represents a single data element and can be displayed in three forms:

A. **Line**

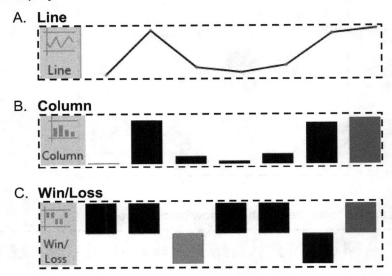

B. **Column**

C. **Win/Loss**

Please see chapters 13 & 14 for examples using Sparklines

ICON SETS (CONDITIONAL FORMATTING)

Icon sets are a type of conditional formatting allowing users to visually identify cell values with *a graphic symbol* based on specific criteria, such as thresholds, percentiles, or a formula. The most commonly used indicators are directional **arrows**; positive, negative, neutral **indicators**; and **ratings:**

MONTH 🔽	SALES_$	+/- LAST MONTH	
Jan	$6,181		
Feb	$6,211	⇨	0.5%
Mar	$6,196	⇨	-0.2%
Apr	$6,174	⇨	-0.4%
May	$6,202	⇨	0.5%
Jun	$6,196	⇨	-0.1%
Jul	☆ $5,957	⬇	-3.9%
Aug	☆ $6,240	⬆	4.8%
Sep	$6,236	⇨	-0.1%

Please see chapter 13 *for an examples using Icon Sets*

CHAPTER 13

SOCIAL MEDIA DASHBOARD EXAMPLE

A Marketing manager has asked you to create a weekly dashboard for her to monitor social media trends and to ensure money spent on the different mediums is generating *a minimum of* six views a day. The dashboard should include the following:

- The date, day of the week, and number of views for each medium
- A small chart displaying each medium's weekly trend

The *data is generated from a database query*. You'll receive updated data at the start of every week for the prior week's views. Users will access the dashboard online as well as mobile devices.

WEB ADDRESS & FILE NAME FOR EXERCISE:
https://bentonbooks.wixsite.com/bentonbooks/excel-2019
SocialMediaData.xlsx

Sample data for this chapter, due to space limitations **the entire data set is not displayed**.

	A	B	C
1	DATE	MEDIUM	VIEWS
2	6/9/2019	Facebook	6
3	6/10/2019	Facebook	23
4	6/11/2019	Facebook	9
5	6/12/2019	Facebook	7
6	6/13/2019	Facebook	10
7	6/14/2019	Facebook	22
8	6/15/2019	Facebook	24
9	6/9/2019	Instagram	24
10	6/10/2019	Instagram	22
43	6/15/2019	Twitter	17

PREPARING THE DATA

The dashboard is the end product, however we must first transform the raw data into a format in which graphics may be applied and allows the customer to perform the analysis requested.

First, we'll create a PivotTable to display the data in a tabular layout.

1. Open exercise file SocialMediaData.xlsx and select **columns 'A:C'**

2. From the Ribbon select **Insert : PivotTable**

3. Select the '**New Worksheet**' radio button

4. Click the '**OK**' button

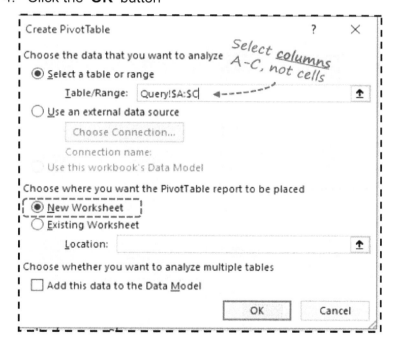

Cells vs Columns
By selecting *columns* instead of *specific cells* we'll be preparing the dashboard to accept new data. When we receive a new week's worth of views we can override our existing dataset and not have to make any additional changes.

5. Rename the new worksheet from **'Sheet1'** to **'Media Dashboard'**

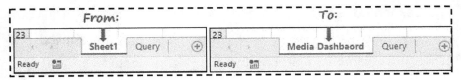

6. In the *'PivotTable Fields' pane* select the following fields:
   - MEDIUM *(Rows section)*
   - DATE *(Columns section)*
   - VIEWS *(∑ Values section)*

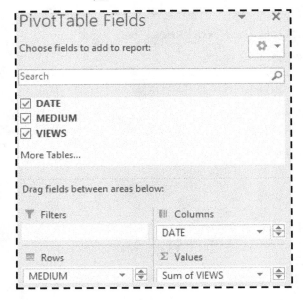

7. Select cell **'J4'**

8. From the **PivotTable Tools** Ribbon select the **'Design'** tab, then the **'Grand Totals'** drop-down arrow

9. Select the option **'On for Columns Only'**

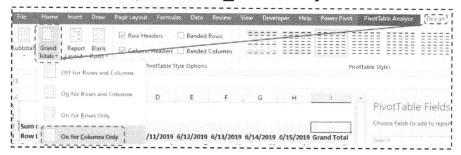

10. Select the drop-down arrow for cell **'B3'** labeled **'Column Labels'** and **uncheck** the box for **(blank)**

11. Click the **'OK'** button

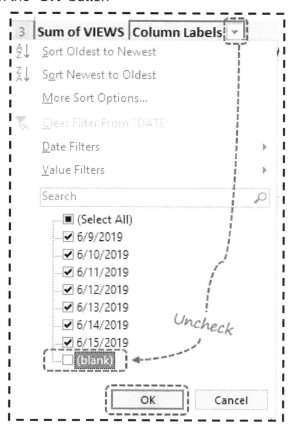

The PivotTable should look similar to the following:

	A	B	C	D	E	F	G	H
1								
2								
3	Sum of VIEWS	Column Labels						
4	Row Labels		6/9/2019	6/10/2019	6/11/2019	6/12/2019	6/13/2019	6/14/2019	6/15/2019
5	Facebook		6	23	9	7	10	22	24
6	Instagram		24	22	28	30	25	16	20
7	LinkedIn		10	9	5	3	4	6	4
8	Reddit		12	10	8	9	9	13	8
9	Tumblr		5	4	13	8	5	10	4
10	Twitter		10	5	7	9	14	13	17
11	Grand Total		67	73	70	66	67	80	77

ADDING SPARKLINES TO THE DASHBOARD

In this section, we'll be adding Sparklines to the dashboard in order to display the trend for the week.

1. **Right-click** on column **'I'**, select '**Column Width…**', set to **45** and **click** the '**OK'** button

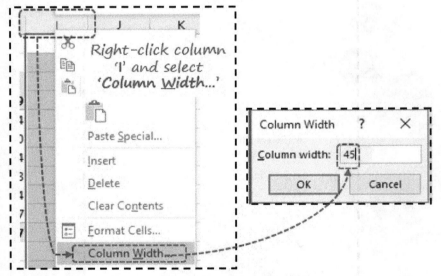

2. Place your cursor in cell **'I5'**, from the Ribbon select **'Insert'**
3. From the '**Sparklines**' menu select **'Line'**

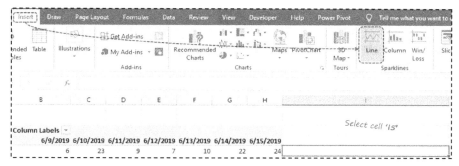

4. In the dialogue box for '**Data Range:**' select cells '**B5:H5**'

5. Click the '**OK**' button

6. With cell '**I5**' active, from the **Ribbon** select the **Sparkline Tools : Design** tab

7. In the '**Show**' section click the '**Markers**' option

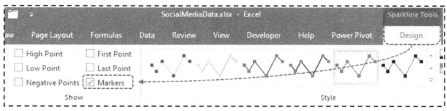

8. Select '**Copy**' or press **Ctrl+C** on your keyboard

9. Copy this formula to cells '**I6:I11**' then press **Ctrl+V** (paste) on your keyboard

10. Press the **Esc (escape)** button on your keyboard

11. Select cell '**I4**' and type '**TREND**'

	A	B	C	D	E	F	G	H	I
2									
3	Sum of VIEWS	Column Labels							
4	Row Labels	6/9/2019	6/10/2019	6/11/2019	6/12/2019	6/13/2019	6/14/2019	6/15/2019	TREND
5	Facebook	6	23	9	7	10	22	24	
6	Instagram	24	22	28	30	25	16	20	
7	LinkedIn	10	9	5	3	4	6	4	
8	Reddit	12	10	8	9	9	13	8	
9	Tumblr	5	4	13	8	5	10	4	
10	Twitter	10	5	7	9	14	13	17	
11	Grand Total	67	73	70	66	67	80	77	

CONDITIONAL FORMATTING & ICON SETS

Next, we'll add visual indicators to assist the viewer with identifying mediums that *are not* generating *the minimum of* six views a day.

1. Select cells **'B5:H10'**

2. From the Ribbon select **Home : Conditional Formatting**

3. Select **'Highlight Cells Rules: Less Than…'**

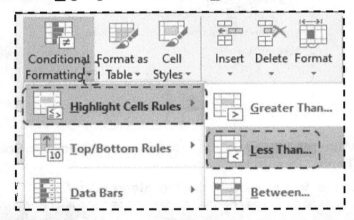

4. For the **'Format cells that are LESS THAN:'** enter the value **6**

5. Click the **'OK'** button

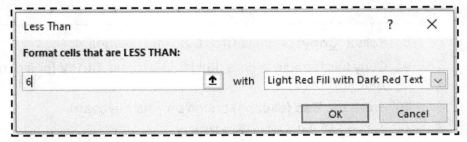

6. Select cells **'B5:H10'**

7. From the Ribbon select **Home : Conditional Formatting**

8. Select **'Icon Sets…'** and the ✓ ◐ ✕ indicators

9. From the Ribbon select **Home : Conditional Formatting**

10. Select **'Manage Rules...'**

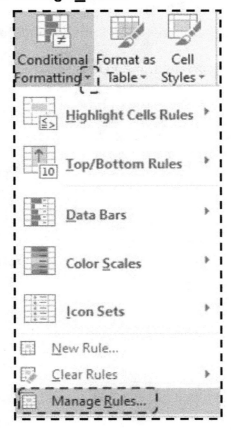

11. Select the **Icon Set** rule

12. Click the **'Edit Rule...'** button

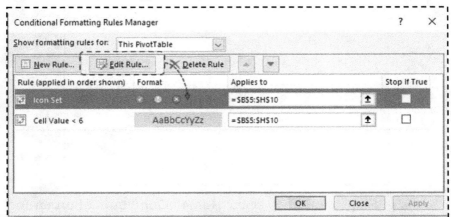

13. Complete the following:
    a. Change the **'Type'** to **Number**
    b. Change the **'Values'** to **6**
    c. Click the drop-down arrow for **'when value is'** and select **'No Cell Icon'**
    d. Click the drop-down arrow for **'when < 6 and'** and select **'No Cell Icon'**
    e. Click the **'OK'** button

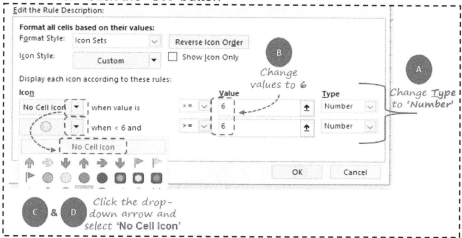

14. Click the **'Apply'** button, then the **'OK'** button

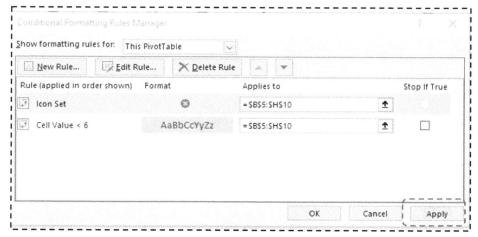

FORMATTING THE DASHBOARD

Lastly, we'll format the dashboard to improve readability.

1. **CHANGE** and **CENTER** the label names:
   - Cell text **'A3'** to **DAILY VIEWS**
   - Cell text **'A4'** to **MEDIUM**
   - Cell text **'B3'** to **DAY**
   - Cell text **'A11'** to **TOTAL**
   - Change the font to **bold** for cell **'I4'**

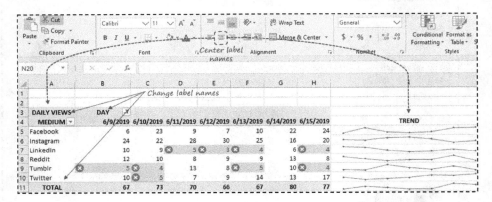

2. Select **row 2**, **right-click**, and select **'Delete'**

3. Select cell **'A1'** and type **'Social Media Trends'**

4. Select cell **'A1'** change the font to **Bold**, **size 22,** and **'Merge & Center'** across columns **'A:I'**

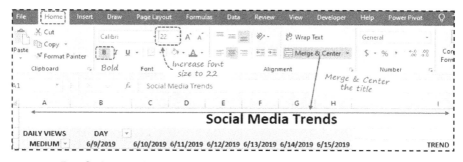

5. Select cells **'A3:I10'**

6. Click the **'Boarders'** drop-down arrow and choose option **'All Boarders'**

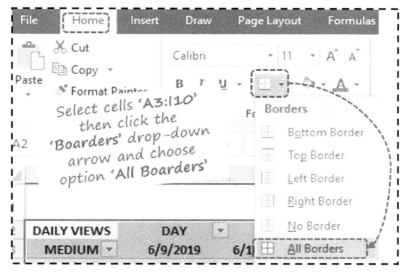

7. Select cells **'A2:I3'** and choose a font shading option of your choice

8. Select cells **'A10:H10'** and choose a font shading option of your choice

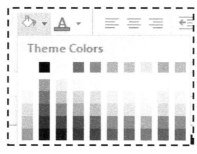

9. Select rows **'4 - 10'** right-click and select **'<u>R</u>ow Height...'**

10. When prompted enter the **'<u>R</u>ow height:'** value **35**

11. Click the **'OK'** button

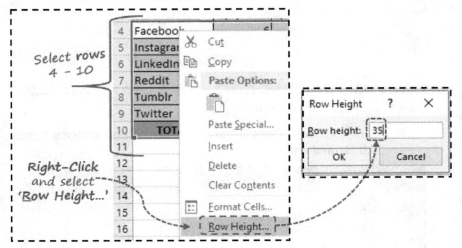

The dashboard should look similar to the following:

DAILY VIEWS	DAY							TREND
MEDIUM	6/9/2019	6/10/2019	6/11/2019	6/12/2019	6/13/2019	6/14/2019	6/15/2019	
Facebook	6	23	9	7	10	22	24	
Instagram	24	22	28	30	25	16	20	
LinkedIn	10	9	5	3	4	6	4	
Reddit	12	10	8	9	9	13	8	
Tumblr	5	4	13	8	5	10	4	
Twitter	10	5	7	9	14	13	17	
TOTAL	67	73	70	66	67	80	77	

Social Media Trends

We've met the customer's requirements of building a weekly dashboard displaying the date, day of the week, and number of views for each medium and each medium's weekly trend.

Please see <u>Chapter 15</u> page 156 to learn more about Refreshing PivotTable Data.

CHAPTER 14

AUTO PARTS DASHBOARD EXAMPLE

The Director of Sales has asked you to create a monthly dashboard for her to ensure auto part sales are on-track to meet monthly and annual targets for four US regions.

The dashboard should include the following for a **YTD** (year-to-date) time period:

- Sales by region
- The total sales compared to plan dollars
- Sales by auto category
- The number of employees *not meeting* their sales goals by 5% or more
- The number of employees *exceeding* their sales goals by 5% or more
- The overall monthly sales trend

The *data is generated from a database query*. You'll receive updated data at the start of every month for the prior month's sales. Users will access the dashboard online, including mobile devices, as well as some users will receive a print-out of the dashboard.

WEB ADDRESS & FILE NAME FOR EXERCISE:
https://bentonbooks.wixsite.com/bentonbooks/excel-2019
Autopart_Sales_Dashboard.xlsx

IMPORTANT!

To save our readers time and to aid in the learning process most *graphics* and *formatting have already been applied* to this exercise file. To learn about how the graphics were added, please see the worksheet named **'Formatting Information'**. *–Thank you!*

Sample data for this chapter, due to space limitations **the entire data set is not displayed**.

	A	B	C	D	E	F	G
1	**REGION**	**EMPLOYEE**	**CATEGORY**	**COMPONENTS**	**EOM_DATE**	**PLAN**	**SALES**
2	Central	Perry, Chloe	Other	Air Bags	31 January 2019	$ 12	$ 11
3	Central	Perry, Chloe	Other	Air conditioning system (A/	31 January 2019	$ 13	$ 11
4	Central	Perry, Chloe	Electrical	Audio/video devices	31 January 2019	$ 13	$ 11
5	Central	Perry, Chloe	Other	Bearings	31 January 2019	$ 13	$ 12
6	Central	Perry, Chloe	Power Train	Braking system	31 January 2019	$ 13	$ 11
7	Central	Perry, Chloe	Structural	Bumper	31 January 2019	$ 13	$ 11
8	Central	Perry, Chloe	Electrical	Cameras	31 January 2019	$ 13	$ 13
9	Central	Perry, Chloe	Interior	Carpet	31 January 2019	$ 13	$ 12
10	Central	Perry, Chloe	Other	Console	31 January 2019	$ 13	$ 12
2881	West	Williams, Jasmin	Electrical	Wiring harnesses	30 June 2019	$ 13	$ 13

You've reviewed the customer's requirements and while they didn't initially ask for the ability to *filter by time period*, you anticipate this is something they may want in the future and therefore decide to design accordingly.

In order to build this Dashboard you will need to:

- Accommodate up-to 12 months of data
- Create 6 PivotTables
- Add 1 Sparkline
- Include 1 pie chart
- Insert 6 icon graphics
- Add 1 Timeline
- Size to fit or be *"shrunk down"* to display on one standard size (8 ½ x 11 inch) piece of paper (landscape)
- Use colors sparingly, as you don't know if the paper form will be printed in color or in black and white ink
- Prepare the dashboard to receive new data and keep the existing formatting

ADDING MULTIPLE PIVOTTABLES TO A SINGLE WORKBOOK

We'll begin by preparing our data for the dashboard. This will involve creating six PivotTables.

PivotTable #1 - Sales By Region

1. Open the Autopart_Sales_Dashboard.xlsx spreadsheet

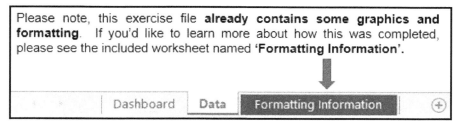

Please note, this exercise file **already contains some graphics and formatting**. If you'd like to learn more about how this was completed, please see the included worksheet named **'Formatting Information'**.

2. Click the **'Data'** tab and select *columns* A:G

3. From the Ribbon select **Insert : PivotTable**

4. When you receive the **Create PivotTable** prompt, select the **'Existing Worksheet'** radio button

5. Place your cursor inside the **'Location:'** box
   - With your cursor still inside the **'Location:'** box click the **'Dashboard'** tab and then cell **'A8'**

The **'Location:'** box should now have **Dashboard!$A$8** entered

6. Click the **'OK'** button

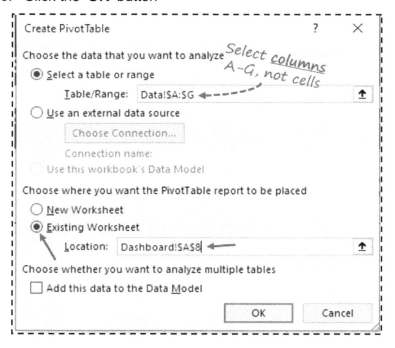

Cells vs Columns
By selecting *columns* instead of *specific cells,* we'll be preparing the dashboard to accept new data. When we receive a new month's worth of sales we can append our existing dataset and not have to make any additional changes.

7. With your cursor in cell **'A8'** of the **'Dashboard'** tab, right-click and select **'PivotTable Options…'**

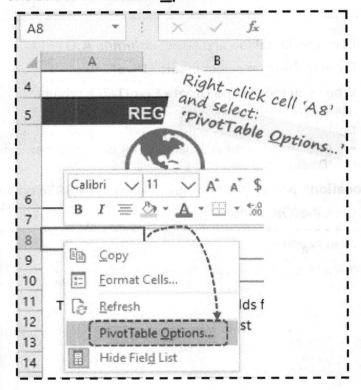

8. Make the following PivotTable Option updates:
   - Enter **'Regions'** for the **PivotTable Name**
   - **Check** the box for **'Merge and center cells with labels'**
   - **Uncheck** the box for **'Autofit column widths on update'**
   - Click the **'OK'** button

PivotTable Options   ? ☐ ✕

PivotTable **N**ame: Regions ◄─────

Layout & Format   Totals & Filters   Display   Printing   Data   Alt Text

Layout

☑ **M**erge and center cells with labels

When in **c**ompact form indent row labels: 1 ⬍ character(s)

Display fields in report filter area: Down, Then Over ∨

Report filter **f**ields per column: 0 ⬍

Format

☐ For **e**rror values show: ☐

☑ For **e**mpty cells **s**how: ☐

☐ **A**utofit column widths on update

☑ **P**reserve cell formatting on update

OK   Cancel

9. In the *'PivotTable Fields' pane* select the following fields:
   - **REGION** *(Rows section)*
   - **SALES** *(∑ Values section)*

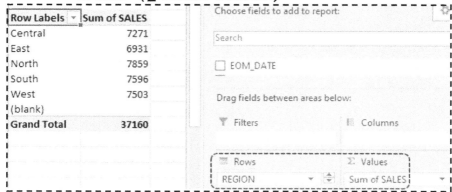

Row Labels ▾	Sum of SALES
Central	7271
East	6931
North	7859
South	7596
West	7503
(blank)	
Grand Total	**37160**

Choose fields to add to report: ⚙

Search

☐ EOM_DATE

Drag fields between areas below:

▼ Filters   ▥ Columns

▥ Rows   ∑ Values

REGION ▾ ⬍   Sum of SALES ▾

10. Format the PivotTable:

- Select cell **'A8'** and change the text from **'Row Labels'** to **'REGIONS'**

- Select cell **'B8'** and change the text from **'Sum of TOTAL'** to **'SALES_$'**

- Select cell **'A15'** and change the text from **'Grand Total'** to **'TOTAL'**

- Select cells **'B9:B14'** and change to a currency format of your choice

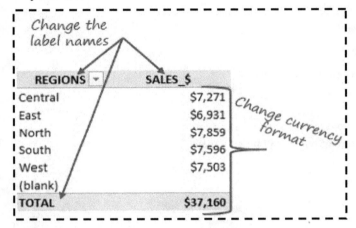

11. Select cell **'A8'**, and then from the **PivotTable Tools** Ribbon select the tab **Design : PivotTable Styles**

12. From the **PivotTable Styles** drop-down, select a format style you like

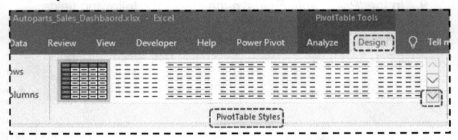

13. Select cells **'A8:B15'** and add borders to the table, from the Ribbon **Home : Font : Boarders drop-down : <u>A</u>ll borders**

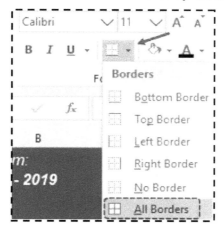

14. Select cell **'A8'**, click the **drop-down arrow** and uncheck the **'(blank)'** option

15. Click the **'OK'** button

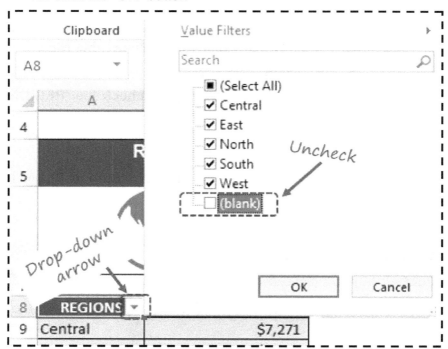

The dashboard should look *similar* to the following:

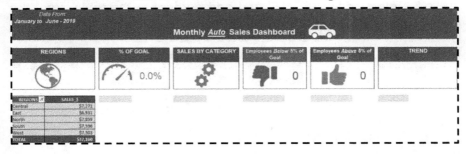

Now that we've built and formatted our first PivotTable *we can reuse* it for the subsequent measures.

PivotTable #2 - % OF GOAL

1. Select cells **'A8:B14'** right-click and select **'Copy'** or press **Ctrl+C** on your keyboard

2. Place your cursor in cell **'D8'** and press **Ctrl+V** (paste) on your keyboard

3. With your cursor in cell **'D8'**, right-click and select **'PivotTable Options…'** enter **'%_Of_Goal'** for the **PivotTable Name**

4. Click the **'OK'** button

5. Inside the *'PivotTable Fields' pane* **uncheck** the **'REGION'** box

6. Inside the *'PivotTable Fields' pane* click the **'PLAN'** box or drag this field to the **'∑ Values'** section

7. Select cell **'E8'** and change the text from **'Sum of PLAN'** to **'PLAN_$'**

8. Select cell **'E9'** and change to a currency format of your choice

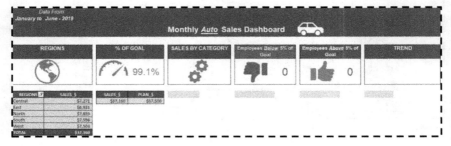

PivotTable #3 – SALES BY CATEGORY

1. Select cells **'D8:E9'** right-click and select **'Copy'** or press **Ctrl+C** on your keyboard

2. Place your cursor in cell **'G8'** and press **Ctrl+V** (paste) on your keyboard

3. With your cursor in cell **'G8'**, right-click and select **'PivotTable Options…'** enter **'Sales_By_Category'** for the **PivotTable Name**

4. Click the **'OK'** button

5. Inside the *'PivotTable Fields' pane* **uncheck** the **'PLAN'** box

6. Inside the *'PivotTable Fields' pane* click the **'CATEGORY'** box or drag this field to the **'Rows'** section

7. Select cell **'G8'** and change the text from **'REGIONS'** to **'CATEGORY'**

8. Select cell **'G8'**, click the **drop-down arrow** and uncheck the **'(blank)'** option

CALCULATED FIELDS

For our next two PivotTables, we'll be using a **custom calculated field**. As demonstrated in the previous chapters, PivotTables have many built-in mathematical features, however the type of analysis you perform may require more complex calculations than those included in the standard set of PivotTable 'Value Field Settings'. This is when the ability to insert your own **'Calculated Fields'** is particularly helpful.

PivotTable #4 – Employees Below 5% OF GOAL

1. Select cells **'G8:H14'** right-click and select **'Copy'** or press **Ctrl+C** on your keyboard

2. Place your cursor in cell **'J8'** and or press **Ctrl+V** (paste) on your keyboard

3. With your cursor in cell **'J8'**, right-click and select **'PivotTable Options…'** enter '**Employees_Below'** for the **PivotTable Name**

4. Click the **'OK'** button

5. Inside the *'PivotTable Fields' pane* **uncheck** the **'CATEGORY'** & **'SALES'** boxes

6. Inside the *'PivotTable Fields' pane* **check** the **'EMPLOYEE'** box

7. Select cell **'J8'** change the name from **'CATEGORY'** to **'EMPLOYEE'**

8. From the **PivotTable Tools** Ribbon select the tab **Design**

9. Click the drop-down box for **'Grand Totals'** and select **'Off for Rows and Columns'**

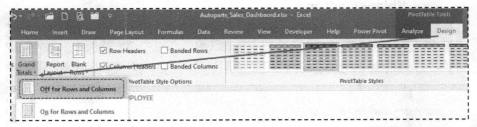

10. From the **PivotTable Tools** Ribbon select the tab **Analyze**

11. Click the **'Fields, Items & Sets'** drop-down box and select **'Calculated Field…'**

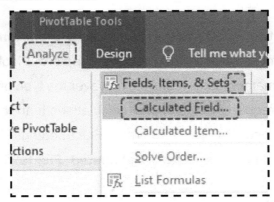

12. In the **Name:** field enter **'%_OF_GOAL**'

13. In the **Formula field:** enter the following formula
$$= (SALES-PLAN)/PLAN$$

14. Click the **'OK'** button

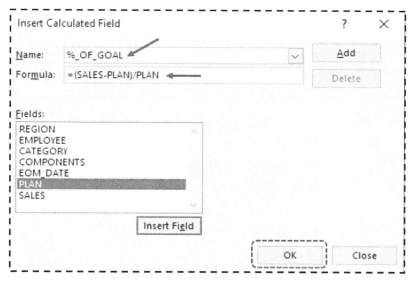

Note: the **'%_OF_GOAL'** field was added to our PivotTable results:

15. Click on the **'Sum of %_OF_GOAL'** drop-down box and select **'Value Field Settings…'**

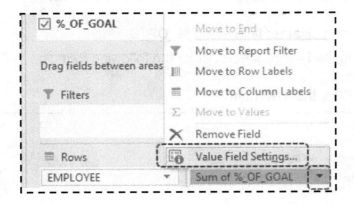

16. In the field **'Custom Name:'** change to **'Sum of %_OF_GOAL'** to **'+/- GOAL'**

17. Click the **'Number Format'** button

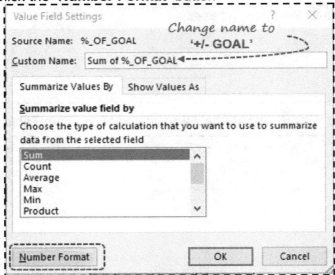

18. Select **'Percentage'** and change **'Decimal places:'** to **1**

19. Click the **'OK'** button *twice*

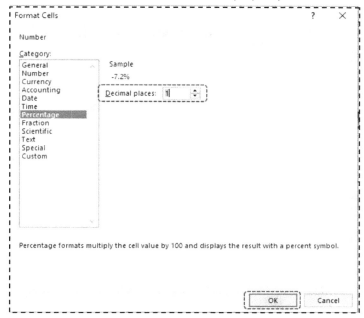

20. Select cell **'J8'**, click the **drop-down arrow** and select '<u>V</u>alue Filters'

21. From the sub-menu select '**Less Than Or Equal To...**'

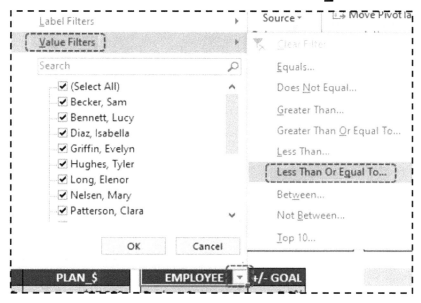

22. The following prompt will appear, enter the number **-0.05** in the field after the drop-down box *'is less than or equal to'*

23. Click the **'OK'** button

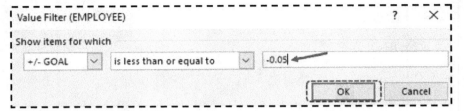

24. Select cell **'J8'**, click the **Filter drop-down arrow** and select **'More Sort Options...'**

25. Click the radio button for **'Ascending (A to Z) by:'**, click the drop-down box and select **'+/- GOAL'**

26. Click the **'OK'** button

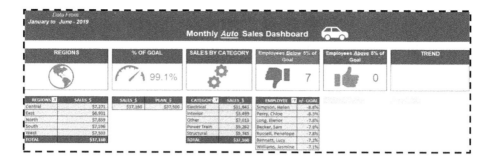

PivotTable #5 – Employees Above 5% OF GOAL

1. Select cells **'J8:K15'** right-click and select **'Copy'** or press **Ctrl+C** on your keyboard

2. Place your cursor in cell **'M8'** and or press **Ctrl+V** (paste) on your keyboard

3. With your cursor in cell **'M8'**, right-click and select **'PivotTable Options...'** enter **'Employees_Above'** for the **PivotTable Name**

4. Click the **'OK'** button

5. Select cell **'M8'**, click the **Filter button drop-down arrow** and select **'Value Filters'**

6. From the sub-menu select **'Less Than Or Equal To...'**

7. The following prompt will appear:
   - Click the second drop-down box and select **'is greater than or equal to'**

   - Enter the number **0.05** in the field after the drop-down box *'is greater than or equal to'*

8. Click the **'OK'** button

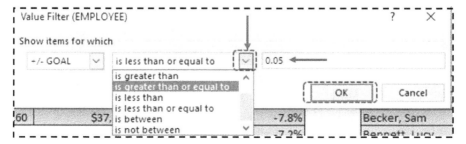

9. Select cell **'M8'**, click the **Filter button** and select **'More Sort Options...'**

10. Click the radio button for **'Descending (Z to A) by:'**

11. Click the **'OK'** button

REMOVING OR CHANGING CALCULATED FIELDS

To remove or change a calculated field:

1. From the **PivotTable Tools** Ribbon select the tab **Analyze**

2. Click the **'Fields, Items & Sets'** drop-down box

3. Select **'Calculated Field...'**

4. In the **'Name:'** drop-down box select the calculated field you would like to change or remove

5. Click appropriate button, either **'Modify'** or **'Delete'**

6. Click the **'OK'** button

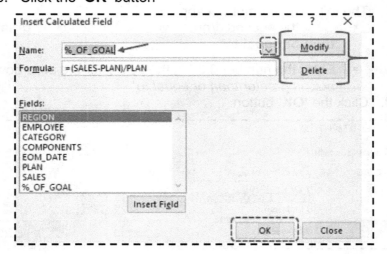

CALCULATED FIELD LIMITATIONS

While calculated fields are helpful, they do have their limitations. The problem is related to **Grand Total calculations**. Most often this occurs when you attempt to multiply two fields in a dataset where some aggregation has already occurred.

For example, when your data contains fields called 'Units' & 'Price' and you attempt to determine the extended price, i.e. Units * Price, the individual rows will calculate correctly. However, the **Totals** will compute as the *SUM of*(Units)*SUM of*(Price).

Let's walk through an illustration, let's say you're attempting to calculate each vehicle type's total sales, however the vehicles were *sold at different prices*.

Aggregated
column

DATE	VEHICLE	UNITS	PRICE
11/28/2019	Car	2	$8,000
11/28/2019	Car	4	$6,000
11/28/2019	Car	6	$5,000
11/28/2019	Truck	2	$16,000
11/28/2019	Truck	4	$12,000
11/28/2019	Truck	6	$10,000

Dataset

You create a PivotTable with a **calculated field** called **'SALES_TOTAL'** which is the units * price, the individual rows are correct, however the totals are not.

VEHICLE ▾	UNITS_SOLD	UNIT_PRICE	SALES_TOTAL	
⊟ Car				
2	2	$8,000	$16,000	Calculated field
4	4	$6,000	$24,000	— correct
6	6	$5,000	$30,000	units * price
Car Total	12	$19,000	$228,000	◄ – – – – – Incorrect
⊟ Truck				
2	2	$16,000	$32,000	Calculated field
4	4	$12,000	$48,000	— correct
6	6	$10,000	$60,000	units * price
Truck Total	12	$38,000	$456,000	◄ – – – – – Incorrect
Grand Total	24	$57,000	$1,368,000	◄ – – – – – Incorrect

Totals are incorrectly
summing the units * sum of price

Microsoft is aware of this issue,[3] however has not provided a timeframe as to when the problem will be fixed.

Let's resume building our auto parts dashboard:

PivotTable #6 – TREND

For our last PivotTable, we'll be working with a date field. We'll be grouping the EOM_DATE by month. In order to work with the date displayed as a month, we'll need to perform some nonintuitive steps.

1. Select cells **'A8:B14'** right-click and select **'Copy'** or press **Ctrl+C** on your keyboard

2. Place your cursor in cell **'P8'** and or press **Ctrl+V** (paste) on your keyboard

---

[3] *Calculated field returns incorrect grand total in Excel, retrieved 18 November 2019 from Microsoft®*
https://support.microsoft.com/en-us/help/211470/calculated-field-returns-incorrect-grand-total-in-excel

3. With your cursor in cell **'P8'**, right-click and select **'PivotTable Options…'** enter **'Trend'** for the **PivotTable Name**

4. Click the **'OK'** button

5. Inside the *'PivotTable Fields' pane* **uncheck** the **'REGION'** box

6. Inside the *'PivotTable Fields' pane* **check** the **'EOM_DATE'** box. *Note: this added an additional field named 'Months'*

7. Inside the *'PivotTable Fields' pane* once the **'Months'** field is added uncheck **'EOM_DATE'**

8. Inside the *'PivotTable Fields' pane* **drag** the **'SALES'** field to the **'Σ Values'** section

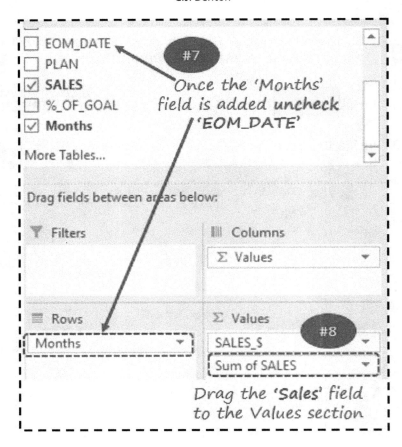

9. Click on the **'Sum of SALES'** drop-down arrow and select **'Value Field Settings…'**

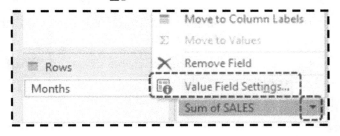

10. From the **'Value Field Settings'** prompt:

- Select the tab '**Show values as**'
- For the **'Show values as'** drop-down list select '% Difference From'
- Select **Base field:** Months & **Base item:** (previous)
- Change the **'Number Format'** to a percent with one decimal place
- For **'Custom Name:'** enter '+/- LAST MN'
- Click the **'OK'** button

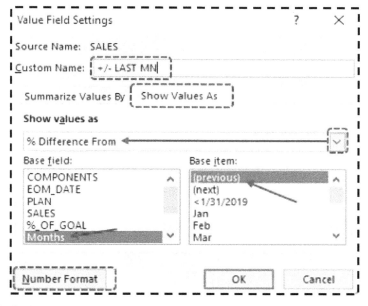

11. Select cell **'P8'** and change the text from **'REGIONS'** to **'MONTH'**

12. From the **PivotTable Tools** Ribbon select the tab **Design**

13. Click the **'Grand Totals'** drop-down box and select **'Off for Rows and Columns'**

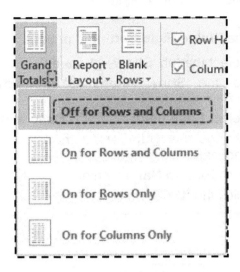

ADDING SPARKLINES TO THE DASHBOARD

1. Place your cursor in cell **'P6'**, from the Ribbon select **'Insert'**
2. From the '**Sparklines**' sub-menu select **'Win/Loss'**

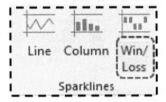

3. In the dialogue box for **'Data Range:'** select cells **'R10:R22'**
   (we're preparing to eventually receive 12 months of data)
4. Click the **'OK'** button

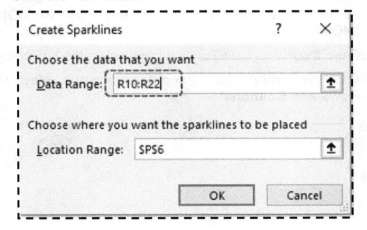

5. Select cells **'P6:R6'**, then from the Ribbon select **HOME :
Merge & Center**

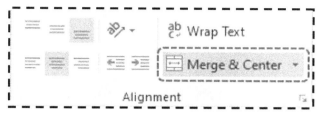

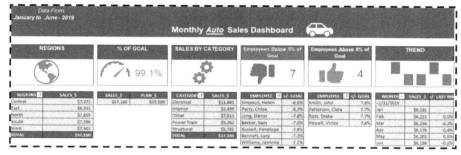

ADDING A CHART TO THE DASHBOARD

1. Select cells **'G9:H13'** and from the Ribbon select **PivotTable
Tools : Analyze** and then the **PivotChart** icon

2. Select the **'Pie'** option

3. Click the **'OK'** button

4. **Move** the chart below the '**REGIONS'** PivotTable (cell **'A17'**)

5. **Expand** the **length & width** to allow for easier viewing

6. Hide the **Field buttons**, **right-click** over any **Field button** and
select **'Hide All Field Buttons on Chart'**

7. Click on the Pie chart and from the **PivotChart Tools** Ribbon
select the tab **Design**

8. Click the drop-down for **'Quick Layout'** and then **'Layout 1'**

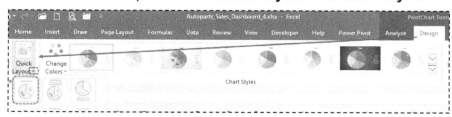

9. Change the color scheme, to the fifth blue Monochromatic option

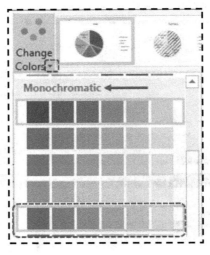

10. Change the chart title from **'Total'** to **'% of Sales by Category'**

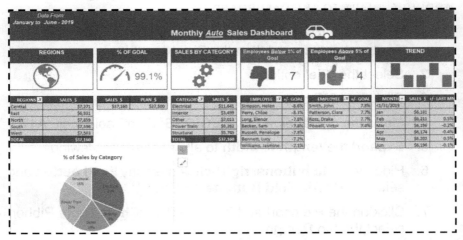

ADDING A TIMELINE TO THE DASHBOARD

The final piece of dashboard is to include a Timeline allowing users to easily view different time periods.

1. Select cell **'P8'** and from the Ribbon select **PivotTable Tools : Analyze** and then **'Insert Timeline'**

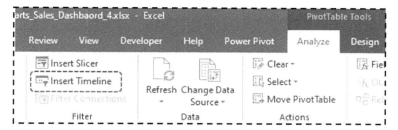

2. The following prompt will appear, click the **'EOM_DATE'** box

3. Click the **'OK'** button

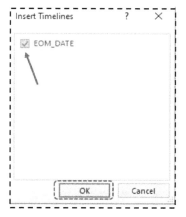

4. Drag the **Timeline** to the area near cell **'G17'**

REPORT CONNECTIONS

5. **Right-click** on the newly added Timeline and from the pop-up menu select **'Report Connections…'**

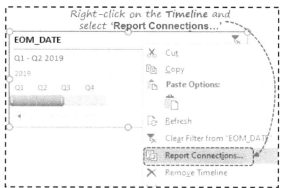

6. When prompted, select _all_ checkboxes

7. Click the **'OK'** button

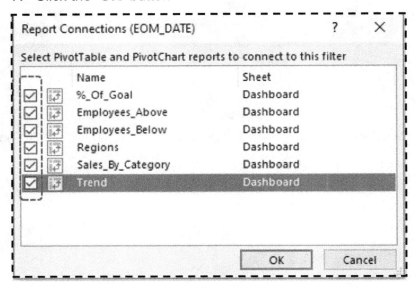

8. From the **Timeline Tools** Ribbon under **'Options'** go to **'Caption'** and enter the new name of **'Time Frame'** *(for detailed instructions on how to change captions please see* chapter 9 page 41*)*

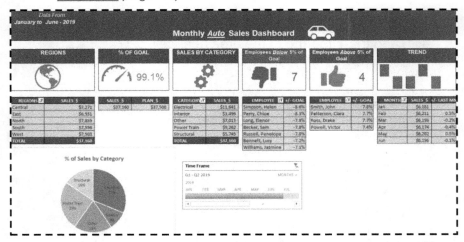

In the next chapter *we'll review how to refresh PivotTable and dashboard data.*

CHAPTER 15

REFRESHING PIVOTTABLE AND DASHBOARD DATA

Once you have created a PivotTable and/or Dashboard with the preferred layout and formatting, you're ready to receive new data.

New information may be added to your existing PivotTable(s) either by appending or overwriting the existing data using the **Refresh** feature. Refreshing your data, allows you to keep your current formatting and calculations. Just remember in your initial design to allow for additional rows and columns that may be created when appending records.

WEB ADDRESS & FILE NAME FOR EXERCISE:
https://bentonbooks.wixsite.com/bentonbooks/excel-2019
Autoparts_Sales_Refresh_Data.xlsx

APPENDING AN EXISTING (INTERNAL) DATA SOURCE

In our first example, we'll review using the **Refresh** feature by appending records. If you recall in chapter 14 the Auto Parts Dashboard, we created the initial PivotTable by selecting columns and not specific cells. Thus, we can receive a new month's worth of sales and append our existing dataset, while continuing to keep all of our existing formatting and calculations.

1. Open the Autoparts_Sales_Refresh_Data.xlsx worksheet
2. Select the **'Data'** tab
3. **Copy** cells **'I2:O1441'** by pressing **(CTRL+C)** on your keyboard or:

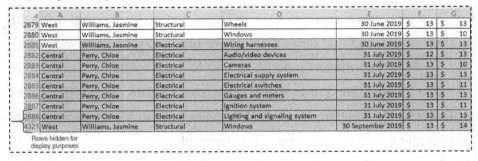

G	H	I	J	K	L	M	N	O
SALES		Data for refresh						
$ 11		Central	Perry, Chloe	Electrical	Audio/video devices	31 July 2019	$ 12	$ 13
$ 11		Central	Perry, Chloe	Electrical	Cameras	31 July 2019	$ 13	$ 10
$ 11		Central	Perry, Chloe	Electrical	Electrical supply system	31 July 2019	$ 13	$ 13
$ 12		Central	Perry, Chloe	Electrical	Electrical switches	31 July 2019	$ 13	$ 11
$ 11		Central	Perry, Chloe	Electrical	Gauges and meters	31 July 2019	$ 13	$ 13
$ 11		Central	Perry, Chloe	Electrical	Ignition system	31 July 2019	$ 13	$ 11
$ 13		Central	Perry, Chloe	Electrical	Lighting and signaling system	31 July 2019	$ 13	$ 13

4. Place your cursor in cell **'A2882'** and press **(CTRL+V)** on your keyboard

	A	B	C	D	E	F	G
2879	West	Williams, Jasmine	Structural	Wheels	30 June 2019	$ 13	$ 13
2880	West	Williams, Jasmine	Structural	Windows	30 June 2019	$ 13	$ 10
2881	West	Williams, Jasmine	Electrical	Wiring harnesses	30 June 2019	$ 13	$ 13
2882	Central	Perry, Chloe	Electrical	Audio/video devices	31 July 2019	$ 12	$ 13
2883	Central	Perry, Chloe	Electrical	Cameras	31 July 2019	$ 13	$ 10
2884	Central	Perry, Chloe	Electrical	Electrical supply system	31 July 2019	$ 13	$ 13
2885	Central	Perry, Chloe	Electrical	Electrical switches	31 July 2019	$ 13	$ 11
2886	Central	Perry, Chloe	Electrical	Gauges and meters	31 July 2019	$ 13	$ 13
2887	Central	Perry, Chloe	Electrical	Ignition system	31 July 2019	$ 13	$ 11
2888	Central	Perry, Chloe	Electrical	Lighting and signaling system	31 July 2019	$ 13	$ 13
4321	West	Williams, Jasmine	Structural	Windows	30 September 2019	$ 13	$ 14

Rows hidden for
display purposes

5. Return to the **'Dashboard' tab** and select cell **'A8'**

6. From the **PivotTable Tools** Ribbon select the tab **Analyze**

7. Click the **'Refresh'** drop-down arrow and select **'Refresh All'**

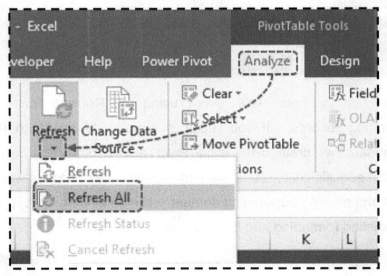

Note: the updated information:

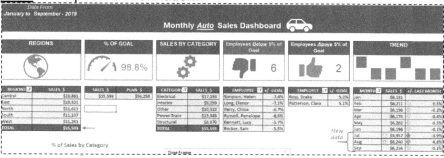

REFRESH VS. REFRESH ALL

The difference between selecting **'Refresh'** vs. **'Refresh All'** is **'Refresh'** only updates the ***active*** PivotTable, by selecting **'Refresh All'** we're updating all of the PivotTables in the Dashboard.

OVERRIDING EXISTING DATA (MANUALLY)

In chapter 13 the Social Media Dashboard our requirements were to display the most recent week's data and not a cumulative view. The process to override data is similar to appending, however with the additional step of deleting the existing data before adding the new records.

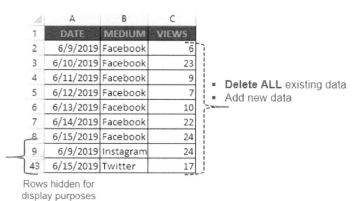

- **Delete ALL** existing data
- Add new data

Rows hidden for display purposes

IMPORTANT!
When overriding records always make sure to completely delete all of the old data before adding the new information.

The process of removing the old information and adding the new can be completed manually or automatically using VBA (<u>V</u>isual <u>B</u>asic for <u>A</u>pplications).

After the above is complete, you would follow the same process of:

- Selecting a cell in the PivotTable

- Then from the **PivotTable Tools** Ribbon select the tab **Analyze**

- Clicking the **'Refresh'** drop-down arrow and selecting **'Refresh <u>A</u>ll'**

REFRESHING DATA FROM AN EXTERNAL SOURCE

In chapters 10 & 11 we created our PivotTable reports from imported data by connecting to external files. If we had saved the reports and then re-opened them we *may* receive the following message:

!SECURITY WARNING External Data Connections have been disabled

This is not a concern as long as the file being opened is from a trusted source. We would click the **'Enable Content'** button and then to refresh these reports we may follow the same process of:

- Selecting a cell in the PivotTable

- Then from the **PivotTable Tools** Ribbon select the tab **Analyze**

- Clicking the **'Refresh'** drop-down arrow and selecting **'Refresh <u>A</u>ll'**

IMPORTANT!
Never open or download files from a **non-trusted** source

Alternatively, you may also refresh the data by:

- From the Ribbon select **Data**
- Select the **'Refresh'** drop-down arrow and then choose the option **'Refresh All'**

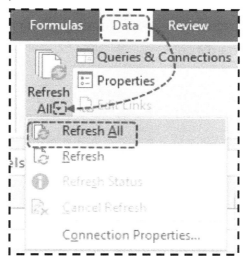

When refreshing from external sources you do not need to delete any existing data. The records will automatically be overwritten with the up-to-date information.

Depending on your audience, you may want to consider *protecting* your Dashboard to prevent unauthorized users from modifying it. As well as, *hide* any data source tabs, thus only allowing your customers to see the Dashboard itself.

IMPORTANT!
Protecting the workbook or worksheet **disables** the use of slicers and prevents users from manually refreshing the data.

WEB ADDRESS & FILE NAME FOR EXERCISE:
https://bentonbooks.wixsite.com/bentonbooks/excel-2019
Autoparts_Sales_Refresh_Data.xlsx

CONCEALING YOUR PIVOTTABLE SOURCE DATA

1. Open the Autoparts_Sales_Refresh_Data.xlsx **worksheet**

2. To *hide* the '**Data**' worksheet, **right click** over the tab and select '**Hide**' from the pop-up menu

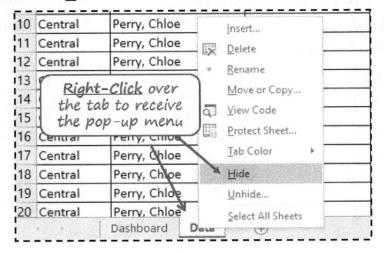

3. From the Ribbon select **Review : Protect Workbook**

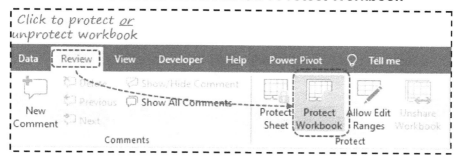

The following dialogue box will appear:

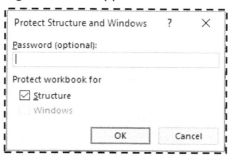

4. Optionally, enter a **Password** or leave blank

5. Click the **'OK'** button

-   To remove the **Protect Workbook Lock**, you would repeat step #3

-   Then to *unhide* the worksheet tab, **right click** over any tab and select **'Unhide...'** *(the 'Unhide...' option will become active once a tab is hidden)*

PROTECTING THE DASHBOARD OR ANY OTHER WORKSHEET

While protecting the workbook protects users from accessing the hidden tabs, it does not prevent them from making changes to the remaining visible worksheets or from refreshing or changing the data source. Therefore, we must complete additional steps:

1. Select the **'Dashboard'** worksheet

2. From the Ribbon select **Review : Protect Sheet**

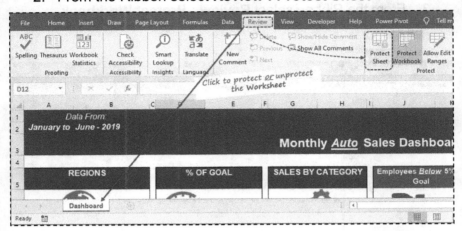

The following dialogue box will appear:

3. You may enter a password or leave blank

4. A good best practice is to leave the first two check boxes selected:
   - Select locked cells
   - Select unlocked cells

These will allow your customers to click on cells and scroll, but not change any content

5. Click the **'OK'** button

If a user tries to modify the sheet, they will receive the one of the
following messages:

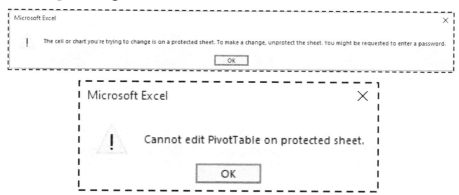

- To **unprotect**, the sheet from the Ribbon select **Review :
  Unprotect Sheet**

Thank you!

Your opinion?

Thank you for purchasing and reading this book, we hope you found it helpful! Your feedback is valued and appreciated! Please take a few minutes and leave a review.

MORE BOOKS AVAILABLE FROM THIS AUTHOR

For a complete list please visit us at:
https://bentonbooks.wixsite.com/bentonbooks/buy-books

- Excel® 2019 VLOOKUP The Step-By-Step Guide
- Excel® 2016 The 30 Most Common Formulas & Features - The Step-By-Step Guide
- Excel® 2016 The VLOOKUP Formula in 30 Minutes The Step-By-Step Guide
- The Step-By-Step Guide To The VLOOKUP formula in Microsoft Excel® *(version 2013)*
- Excel® Macros & VBA For Business Users - A Beginners Guide

QUESTIONS / FEEDBACK

Email: bentontrainingbooks@gmail.com
Website: https://bentonbooks.wixsite.com/bentonbooks